Education and the Concept of Mental Health

THE STUDENTS' LIBRARY OF EDUCATION

Contents

1
Introduction

It is almost impossible for anyone connected with the world of education to avoid having some views, however primitive or uninformed, about mental health : just as it is almost impossible for an intelligent citizen of the western world to avoid having some kind of attitude towards such notions as democracy, freedom and social justice. Further, not many of us would deny that we ought to know more about such things : not just because they are fashionable, or because we want to appear well-informed, or because we have to pass examinations in them, or even because it is our duty as citizens or teachers to know about them, but because they seem to us *important*. Knowing more about mental health or democracy is not (we dimly feel) like knowing more about wild flowers, chess, or the nesting habits of the crested grebe.

We are right to feel this : but for two rather different reasons. There are some things which are important for the community as a whole, but which need not be a matter of deep concern or prolonged study for every individual in the community. For instance, electric power and agriculture are important for our nation, in a sense in which wild flowers and chess are not; but this does not mean that we ought all to be electricians or expert farmers. But there are other things which are important for every individual, and which individuals have to practise for themselves : such things as religion, morality and personal relationships are of this kind. They cannot, in their very nature, be left to experts in the way we can leave electricity and agriculture to experts.

I want to stress from the start that mental health falls into both these categories. We may read in the papers that a high proportion of hospital beds is occupied by the mentally ill: that somebody from every one family in six suffers from mental illness: that mental illness costs the country a great deal of money. This certainly gives it one kind of importance: but, however concerned we may be about the dangers to our community, we may still be tempted to leave it to 'the government' or 'the experts'. On the other hand, if our notion of mental health is (in this respect) more like our notion of religion or morality than it is like our notion of electricity or agriculture, we shall see that it is impossible to shrug off responsibility in this way. On similar grounds (though, as I shall argue, to a lesser extent) the notion of physical health is important to every individual: for physical health is something which, to some degree, individuals have to cultivate for themselves—it cannot be handed to them on a plate by doctors or other experts.

The reader will observe that we have already started to talk about the *concept* of mental health: about what sort of thing it is, and what sort of importance it has: about what it *means* to say that someone is mentally ill, and in what respects this is like or unlike saying that he is physically ill. This is what the present book is about; and it is worth trying to say why this sort of enquiry is important. First, even if mental health were something we could leave to experts, we should want to know just *what it was* that we were leaving to them: we should want, for instance, to be reasonably sure that the experts did not trespass beyond their proper bounds—and we could only be sure by knowing what their proper bounds were: that is, by knowing what mental health was. (In the same way, we might want to leave economics to economists: but, though we want their advice, we don't want them to go beyond their expertise and tell us how to live in all respects—and so we have to know what economics

2

is, what is a purely economic question and what isn't.) But secondly, if mental health is something which is important to each of us as individuals, then it is at least possible that we all ought to know something about what it is. Of course a man can be mentally healthy without knowing what mental health is, just as he can be happy without knowing what happiness is: but a prudent man would learn as much as possible about it, so as to be better equipped to preserve it or acquire more of it.

For these reasons, this book will not be chiefly concerned with the facts about mental health, but with the concept of mental health in relation to education. Indeed, it seems exceedingly dangerous to speak too lightly of 'the facts' about mental health, if we are not already clear what mental health is: for how are we to know whether they are facts about mental health or something quite different? For instance, there are some societies in which it might be thought mad to believe in devils, and others in which it might be thought mad not to believe in them. We could find out the statistics (in either society) about this, postulate causes, suggest cures, and so forth: but this might be nothing to do with mental health at all—only with what each society *thought* to be mental health.

This also shows why we must first be clear about the concept, before we can get down to the facts. For part of the point of getting down to facts is to take some practical action—to teach children in a different way, create new sorts of school, train teachers differently, perhaps hire more psychologists, and so forth. But all this might be very dangerous if we are not clear about what we are doing. Again, in some societies it might be thought mad to marry someone of another colour, or not to believe in the established religion or the dominant political party: but we should rightly object if society tried forcibly to 'cure' those who did these things, or even if society strongly suggested to them that they were mad, unless we had been rationally convinced that they really

3

were mad. And to convince somebody rationally involves conceptual clarity as well as factual knowledge.

I believe it to be particularly important for teachers and other educators to be clear in the way described above. If mental health is important for every individual, as I have suggested, then teachers must be particularly alive to what mental health is. For they, more perhaps than anyone else, are concerned with shaping individuals: with turning children, who are potentially adults, into genuine adults. If mental health were like knowing about electricity or agriculture—essential knowledge for certain individuals who are going to do certain jobs, and essential for the community as a whole—then only those teachers who taught those individuals need bother very seriously about it. But if it is like morality or religion, then obviously it is likely that every teacher has a part to play: and he cannot play that part well if he is confused about what he is trying to do.

There are perhaps two general factors which may prevent teachers from clearing up that confusion. The first is the tendency, which we all share except insofar as we consciously fight against it, to take for granted the common views of our society about mental health. There are words which most of us use—'neurotic', 'schizophrenic', 'inferiority complex', and so on—which cover a multitude of sins: and it is in itself significant that we have an immense number of synonyms or near-synonyms for 'mad' or 'mentally ill'—'loony', 'dotty', 'batty', 'nuts', 'round the bend', 'crazy', 'off his head' and many others. The second is the way in which educational institutions are arranged in our society, and the social role which teachers and other educators are expected to play in consequence. These two factors are of course closely interlinked: but institutions tend to lead a life of their own, and do not always immediately reflect public opinion —much less the opinions of those who work in them.

We shall begin, therefore, by considering these two fac-

4

tors. The bulk of the book will then be concerned with clarifying the concept of mental health: we shall have to take a step backwards, as it were, and consider the way we think and act in education from a more detached point of view. Finally we shall make some practical suggestions which seem to follow from the concepts we have clarified. The reader who is unfamiliar with that style of thought which is often called 'philosophy' or 'conceptual analysis' may find himself having to think in a new way. There is no substitute for conceptual clarity, no short cut to getting clear, and no possibility of 'looking up the answers in the back': the subject we are engaged on is not of that kind. But I hope to convince the reader that the hard thinking involved is worth it: and this is, in the long run, more important than whether he agrees or disagrees with any particular points.

2

The present situation

The influence of science

There have always been people who were mentally ill.
But many, perhaps most, societies in the past looked on
such people in what we ourselves could regard as an
'unscientific' way. A madman might be regarded as possessed by devils or afflicted by God: sometimes, in those
societies where the strangeness of lunacy was regarded
with peculiar reverence, as inspired or singled out by God.
Primitive peoples today may drill a hole in a man's skull
'to let out the evil spirits', reminding us of the way in
which doctors in the past might let a patient's blood
'to purge the noxious humours'.

It is often difficult to say how far these primitive ideas
functioned as *explanations* of why a person behaved in
a mad way, and how far they should be taken as *descriptions* of what it feels like to be mad. Even today people
often say things like 'Something is snapping in my head',
'There's a heavy weight pressing down on me', 'It's as if I
were two different people', and so on: and the picture
of being 'possessed by devils', with which we are familiar
in the New Testament and elsewhere, may be quite a
good description of certain mental cases, from the patient's
viewpoint. People with delirium tremens 'see' the snakes
and cockroaches that alcoholism induces: those with
persecution mania 'know' that their closest friends are
plotting against them, or that Martians are attacking them
with radio waves.

As explanations, however, we currently reject such

pictures. Indeed we pride ourselves on our freedom from the 'unscientific' approach which they imply. 'Devils', 'spirits', 'sickness of the soul' and 'demonic possession' are not part of our world-picture. Whatever the causes for this change in attitude—and such things as the decline in religious belief and the success of the natural sciences are certainly connected with it—our own picture appears to be very different. We have—so we believe—a sensible and realistic attitude to mental health as to physical health : we have doctors, psychologists and other scientists to treat those we call 'sufferers' or 'patients' in hospitals and mental wards : we no longer blame the victims of mental 'diseases', and we may even feel that we ought not to look down on them any more than we should look down on people suffering from cancer or diabetes—though in practice we rarely live up to this high-minded belief. All this seems to be a matter for self-congratulation : and if we feel any deficiency on our part, it is apt to be expressed by our saying that not enough is 'being done' for the mentally ill—just as we might say that not enough is being done for the victims of a flood or an earthquake.

This way of looking at things has, however, certain dangers. We may find ourselves rejecting 'devils' or 'evil spirits', but substituting some other picture which looks more 'scientific' but isn't. We do, in fact, find ourselves using words and phrases which suggest that the mind of a man is like a machine, and which suggests the influence of such sciences as mechanics, physics and chemistry. We say 'There's a screw loose somewhere', 'He's had a nervous breakdown', 'She needs her head examined' or 'He's not all there', as if some bit of machinery had broken or was missing. Even though we may admit that such ways of talking are metaphorical or 'not to be taken literally', they nevertheless dominate our thinking. Thus when we talk of an 'inferiority complex' or a 'neurosis', we are apt to think of these as *things* which people *have in their heads*, just as they may have a brain tumour in their

7

heads. This is not much of an improvement on the idea of primitive peoples that evil spirits live inside the skull: as an explanation, it seems naïve.

As a model for description of what madness is like, the 'scientific' machine-picture of the mind seems to do madness even less justice than the old picture in terms of spirits and devils. A person who is pathologically guilty or anxious, for instance, does not characteristically say 'Dear me, my guilt-mechanism is working too hard today, what a nuisance', in the way that a rheumatic might say 'Dear me, my rheumatism is giving me a lot of trouble today'. He says 'I feel that if I do such-and-such, I shall be punished for it' or (in an extreme case) 'God will strike me down'. The old picture retains the personal element, as the modern pseudo-scientific picture does not, in two ways. First, it shows the *man himself* feeling in a certain way, not just noting the fact that there is something wrong with his brain; and secondly, it suggests that the causes of his feelings are concerned with other *people*, not just with pieces of brain-mechanism which have come adrift.

We shall return to these points later. Here I want to suggest only that we must take the 'scientific' attitude— which dominates our thinking far more than we suspect— with a pinch of salt. It may work very well for electricity and planets, for objects in the natural world, but it may not work at all well for human beings. Human beings have *minds* as well as *brains*: and the two are not in the same logical category. The chief interest, as well as the chief difficulty, with the concept of mental health is that it is plainly relevant to both categories, and that we need to see just how it relates to them.

Educational institutions

In general, the way in which the educational organisation of this country functions in relation to mental health can be seen to correspond with the 'scientific' view of mental health which we have just considered. We make a fairly sharp distinction between teachers and doctors. Teachers, we think, have the job of *educating*: they teach Latin, mathematics, French and so forth. Doctors have the job of *curing*: they dress wounds, take out appendices, remove inferiority complexes and give shock-treatment to manic-depressive cases. Again, everybody needs educating; but not everybody is mentally ill. So everybody needs a teacher; but it is only when you are mentally ill—when something goes wrong with you—that you need to worry about your mental health.

Consequently the normal, universal type of institution for young people is not supposed to be concerned with mental health, except insofar as mental illness may incapacitate the clientèle from learning what they are supposed to learn in such an institution. It is tempting to mark this distinction by confining the word 'education' to the transmission of those subjects that teachers teach—Latin, mathematics, etc.—and excluding from the concept of education those processes or activities that might more properly be considered under other titles, of which 'curing' is one.[1] However, this is to beg an important question about what actually happens during processes which we often *call* 'curing' (such as psychoanalysis), and about whether 'education' can be confined in this way. We must also remember that 'curing' is only one such activity. Words like 'punishing', 'reforming', 're-educating', 'character-building', 'inspiring' and (in reference to religion) 'converting' all represent things that go on in institutions of various kinds—Borstals, boarding schools of a certain type, religious seminaries, and so forth. Without a clearer idea of exactly what these words mean—what sort of processes they describe—we should be hesitant before excluding them from the notion of education altogether. It is better to leave the matter open at this stage.

In general, however, this uncertainty is not reflected in

[1] (See Peters, 1966, Part I: also Peters, 1964.)

ECMH—B

our educational institutions, or at least not in what we normally call 'schools'. It is truistic to point out that children go to school to learn subjects and to pass examinations. If they learn them well and pass a lot of examinations, we commonly call them 'well-educated' or at least 'cultured': at any rate they are not 'ignorant' When the school finds its task impossible, or interrupted, by reason of the child having something wrong with him, it may be obliged to call in an expert to put the matter right, or (if that fails) to remove the child altogether. Toothache is dealt with by the school dentist, influenza by the school doctor. Following this pattern, ordinary schools tend to lump together other children with other difficulties under such headings as 'maladjusted', 'spastic', 'autistic', 'retarded', and 'delinquent', and either call in experts to mend them, or else have them removed to special institutions where experts will cater for them.

Yet the picture is more confused than I have presented it, and various features combine to make one wonder whether this sharp distinction is as sharp as it seems. Firstly, we may notice a tradition which precedes the 'scientific' approach, and has survived through it: the tradition that teachers should have something to do with the *sort of person* the child will become, other than just in the sense that he may end up as more or less 'well-educated' or 'ignorant'. The old phrase 'godliness *and* good learning' represents two different ideals: a man may have learnt a lot and still be ungodly, just as he may have passed a great many examinations and still be a swine. Note that this tradition is not just concerned with what is often called the 'socialisation' of the child: that is, with ensuring that he is a good mixer, knows what the law of the land is, and can make the gestures and motions appropriate to his society. It is concerned with the child as an individual, who may perhaps be living in a society whose standards he ought to reject. To be 'godly' or to be a 'true revolutionary' may well, for Christians and Communists

10

respectively, entail being the sort of person who fights against social standards at a particular time.

Secondly, the decline in the importance and authority of the family in recent years has meant that the school has taken on a number of functions which go beyond its teaching task. It ensures that the children are clean and hygienic, that they are properly fed at school, and that they do not get into trouble with the police. The school is also partly responsible for seeing that the children actually *go* to school; and this, combined with its other social functions, means that some degree of liaison with the parents is inevitable. In practice, and to an increasing extent, notions like 'being a teacher', 'child welfare', 'social work' and many others are found to overlap; and it is becoming more and more difficult for a teacher to confine himself entirely to teaching his subject, and to exclude the feelings, motives, and general background of his pupils entirely from his consideration.

Thirdly, there are still a large number of schools which are overtly dedicated to instilling particular ideals, and have never been content with only teaching subjects. Here the tradition mentioned above survives in a purer form. We need only think of some of the boarding-schools whose spiritual father was Dr. Arnold; of sectarian religious schools, such as the Roman Catholic schools or the Quaker schools; and of the modern 'progressive' schools whose ideals, though often somewhat more vaguely expressed, plainly include more than 'education' in the purely social or intellectual sense. These are not thought, by those who control or work in them, to be 'special schools' in the way that Borstals or schools for maladjusted children are: nor do they always claim that only a certain type of child is suitable for education in their institution—still less that only children who are in some respect underprivileged are suitable.

All this should make us at least hesitate before we accept any slick view about 'the function' of a school, or 'the job' of a teacher. Because of the pressure put on us, partly by the jobs we have to do, and partly by the way in which most people think (or uncritically accept things), we are tempted to think that there is such a thing as 'the function' of a school, written ineradicably, as it were, into the book of nature: and such a thing as 'the job' of a teacher, as if this were not something that could be changed. Whatever the important differences in meaning between such concepts as 'teaching' and 'mental health', these conceptual differences themselves must not be allowed to control our practical affairs: they can only clarify them. Jobs and institutions are made by men, and can be changed by men.

Pressures on the practising teacher

So far we have mentioned only what one might call conceptual pressures on the teacher: the way in which society in general thinks about mental health, and the way in which educational institutions are arranged and function in relation to mental health. All this, however, is very abstract, though it is also very important. It would be quite possible for a teacher to think about the concept in quite a different way from his society, and also consciously to resist or disagree with the way in which the function of schools is generally conceived. Indeed, no doubt many practising teachers—and perhaps many more theoretical 'educationalists'—do just this. But they are still subject to practical pressures.

What teachers should or could do about such pressures must be discussed only after we have considered the concept of mental health itself. But the nature of the pressures is worth a brief consideration. They can be divided into five headings: (a) the headmaster and other teachers in the institution, (b) governors of the school or state authorities, (c) parental and public opinion, (d) the expectations of the children themselves, and (e) the examination system.

These tend to reinforce each other, and will be considered together.

In general these five factors combine to force on the teacher a picture of the Ideal Child—the sort of boy or girl that the teacher should be trying to produce. Most headmasters, together with those (often older) teachers who form the 'establishment' of a school, want a boy to be 'a credit to the school' : well-behaved, able to exercise authority by being a prefect or a games captain : courteous and hard-working : if possible, academically successful : above all, not a trouble-maker. The governors or local authorities in their turn—though in Britain they tend to be less powerful than the headmaster—keep a watching brief on the school authorities, and have much the same criteria of success in mind. If the school puts on good plays, wins its matches, gains an adequate amount of 'O' Levels or other academic certificates, gets a good name for being well-mannered and helpful to adults, and so forth, they are satisfied. Parents again, for the most part, want the child to be satisfactorily 'socialised'. This may mean different things to different parents : working-class parents, for instance, may stress the importance of the child acquiring those qualifications that will enable him to get a good job, and middle- or upper-class parents may prefer to emphasise 'gentlemanly behaviour' or 'decent manners'. In most cases, however, it is the public success of the child, rather than his happiness or mental health, which seems most important to them. Fourthly, the children themselves, treated since school-age according to these criteria of success, come to expect that teachers will go on treating them thus; and if a teacher attempts to treat them otherwise, he may meet with resistance, hostility, anxiety or even contempt. Finally, the academic side of these criteria is given form and point by the existence of the examination system, powerful not only because it may affect a pupil's future career but also because, within the school and in the eyes of his fellows and teachers, success or failure in examinations is obviously important to him, and something he cannot hide or evade.

The above is, of course, far too quick an account of the kind of pressures individual teachers have to face. It needs not only filling out, but also toning down by mentioning the many exceptions. Not all headmasters or all parents have these criteria: many boards of governors and local authorities give a very free hand to 'progressive' educators who overtly disown the Ideal Child as what they want to produce: not all children have these impersonal and stereotyped expectations of the teacher: and many schools are not concerned with examinations, or at least are not tied to public examinations in the tight way I have suggested. But in general, the précis I have given is perhaps not too wide of the mark.

A number of other points also combine to sustain this account. First, those institutions which disown the Ideal Child are not usually those in the public eye (unless dragged there by the popular press), or those which cut much ice in the world of affairs. The well-known public boarding schools and the grammar schools are the home of the Ideal Child. If other kinds of ideal children are anywhere recognised, it will be in the 'special' schools, 'ultra-progressive' schools, and schools that some might regard as cranky and all must agree to be nowhere near the top of the educational hierarchy. But, secondly, the image of these other ideal children is not always very clear. A lot of the well-intentioned talk about 'freedom', 'self-expression', 'development of the personality', 'teaching the children to question and rebel', and so forth often expresses little more than a dislike for the Ideal Child. No positive, or at least no conceptually clear, counter-ideal is put forward. And thirdly, as a result of this vacuum the Ideal Child tends to creep back in again. At least his success is clear and measurable; and many a 'progressive' school has turned to more 'establishment' ways, not so much from external pressure as from a desire to produce verifiably good results of *some* kind (rather than just hoping that its children are turning out all right).

Together with this there are a number of even more practical pressures on the teacher. He will, for instance, be allotted a particular classroom, and be paid to teach a certain subject in it at certain specific times of the day. He will have to enforce the code of rules current at the school, and it may be expected of him that he should set a good example in regard to some of them (in matters of dress, 'bad language', sexual behaviour, attitude to religion and so forth). His liaison with the parents may be restricted or controlled by official school policy. The kind of discipline he uses may be restricted or controlled even more: there may be certain set punishments which he must or must not use, for instance. Besides these and other pressures, there is the general consideration that his time and energy will be so taken up by the things he is publicly expected to do, that he will have none left over for any personal ideals of his own which might benefit the children.

Here, too, of course, there may be more scope (particularly for a cunning or strong-minded teacher) than the above implies. Many of the pressures are indirect rather than explicit and a teacher can get away with quite a lot before actually getting the sack. Moreover, there are many posts which are comparatively free from such pressures: and there are even more which, though ostensibly concerned with producing the Ideal Child, can in fact be used to produce Anti-children. The teacher who wants to 'get on', at least in some fields of education, will no doubt do well to yield to or even anticipate the pressures: but education in this country today is in a sufficient state of confusion to admit of multiple possibilities of success. But in general, again, the picture must be recognised for what it is.

From all these points I want to single out the dislike of the Ideal Child, which is being increasingly felt—perhaps particularly by younger teachers and the younger generation as a whole. There is a very strong feeling, in this and such other countries as have some claim to be called 'liberal', that we ought to be producing something else. But, as with the anti-hero in some modern novels, it is fatally easy to construct an Anti-Ideal Child simply by reversing, or rebelling against, the image of the Ideal Child. Is the Ideal Child prejudiced about class and race? Very well, we will produce an Anti-Ideal Child who will assuredly marry out of his own class and whose best friends will be negroes. Does the Ideal Child believe in moral absolutes and the Ten Commandments? The Anti-Ideal Child shall be an existentialist (even if he doesn't know how to spell it) and believe that all moral rules are irrational. If the Ideal Child supports the government, the Anti-Ideal shall be against it: if the one is Christian, the other shall be atheist: if the one highbrow, the other lowbrow.

To react uncritically against prevailing pressures, or to conform uncritically to them, is a poor way of trying to put our (perhaps confused) ideals and interests into practice. The only way forward is to get clearer about what these ideals and interests are, so that teachers can preserve a certain automony of mind throughout their careers. It is in the highest degree unfortunate that teacher-training in the past seems to have failed in this respect, and leaves an immense gulf between theory and practice. Only too often practising teachers, weighed down by the arduous task of having to control too large classes and to get some kind of 'education' into their reluctant heads, look back on their training as 'impractical' or 'unhelpful'. Yet in this country, where educational power is decentralised, it is only if teachers themselves give new ideas an intelligent and practical form that the right sort of changes will be made.

Mental health and educational ideals

All this may seem rather remote from our particular topic.

16

But anyone who takes seriously the whole business of trying to find some new educational ideals, from a dissatisfaction with the prevailing system, will inevitably run up against a number of very confused notions, of which 'mental health' is one of the more fashionable. There are those, indeed, who seem to regard it as *the* single, overall 'aim of education'. It is very easy to be superficially impressed by some particular line of goods in the market of ideals: those, for instance, who are attracted by some glowing notion of 'psychology' or 'psychoanalysis' or unduly influenced by what they take to be the views of Freud, may well seize on 'mental health' as a battle-cry—just as those of a Marxist turn of mind may want to talk about developing the 'social' or 'economic' conscience of the child, or even of educating him to 'play his part in the class struggle'.

We are familiar with many other hazy ideals of this general kind. In the virtually complete confusion of what we call 'religious education', people will be heard to talk of 'a sense of the holy', 'giving the child a faith to live by', 'getting him to think about the meaning of life', and so forth. On others a certain type of literary criticism may have made a great impact: they will talk of 'perception', 'sensitivity' and 'awareness'. Others again, still more hazily desirous that a rigid or formalistic education should give way to wider horizons, will talk of 'creativity' or 'originality'. All these, and many others, express laudable feelings. The appeal of the phrase 'moral education', for instance, is enormous: but consider how differently this might be interpreted by a Roman Catholic, a Communist, a member of the 'old guard' who wants 'more discipline', a rationalist who is concerned that children should not be imposed on or indoctrinated, and so forth.

Once we appreciate this general point, a large number of questions immediately present themselves. Is 'mental health' the whole concern of education? If not, what aspect of the child does it cover? His mind? But presumably the usual curricular subjects which we teach cover that. His brain? But surely that's the concern of doctors and brain-surgeons. His soul? But that's something to do with religious education. His moral attitudes and behaviour? But that must be different from his mental health—it's one thing to be naughty or wicked, and another to be mentally ill. (Or *are* they really different?) Again, is 'mental health' going to be something we teach, like we teach Latin? Or is it to do with the general environment of the family and the school—and if so, how can we improve that environment? How would we measure whether we had improved a child's 'mental health'? Can we examine him in it, and give him marks for it?

Some may perhaps still feel that an unnecessary fuss is being made over something which, in practice, we can identify quite well. 'Surely we know who's mad and who isn't.' Perhaps in some cases we do: but if we do not have a clear grasp of *why we feel entitled to say* that they're mad, we shall not be able to deal with the border-line cases—the psychopathic killers, the 'sex maniacs', the boy who feels compelled to steal things or set fire to things (and is he really *compelled*?). And what about the boy who takes drugs, or the girl who gets pregnant: they may not be 'mad' exactly, but isn't there something wrong with them? Are they really 'mentally healthy'? A young child can't read: is it because he's stupid, or because he's lazy, or because he 'has a mental block' against it (note the machine-metaphor again: perhaps we think of a mental block like a road-block)? And what is the difference between these anyway? Are mad people really mad, or are they just what their society calls mad? (This is like the question 'Is stealing, adultery, etc. really wrong or is it just a matter of what society thinks?')

It is not possible to answer all these questions in a book of this kind; but at least we can try to get clearer about the concept of mental health. All I have tried to show in this introductory chapter is the way in which this enquiry relates to the interests of the teacher, living as he does in a society, and working in social institutions, which already suggest to him certain lines of thought about our topic. What we have now to do is to take a step back from our own opinions, ideals and attitudes—to come down from the clouds of anger, sentiment or heedlessness —and take a long, hard look at the particular concepts with which we are concerned.

3

The concept of mental health

'Health' and 'illness'

What, in general, does it mean to say that somebody is 'ill' or 'well', 'healthy' or 'unhealthy'? It is not easy to be absolutely clear about this; and our best plan will be to list a number of scattered points, and then to draw some general conclusions.

1. It is *people* who are well or ill, not parts of people. We say 'My foot hurts', but not 'My foot is ill'. There are, admittedly, times when we talk differently: we can say 'My cold is better today' or perhaps even 'My foot is completely well now', but we would more naturally say that my cold or my foot were *cured*. Also, though we can talk of 'an unhealthy complexion', 'going for a healthy walk', and so on, these expressions seem to be derived from the prime notion of a person (or a creature of some kind— we should include animals and perhaps plants) being ill. He is ill *because* some part or aspect of him has gone wrong. We must beware, therefore, of talking too lightly about 'a healthy body' or 'a sick mind'.

2. A person is not ill if he is merely *deficient*, or *stunted*, or *missing* in some respect. Midgets and dwarfs are not ill or unhealthy just because they are stunted: nor is an ordinary person ill if he has had his appendix removed, or has only four fingers instead of five on each hand. Even a one-legged man is not *ill*: he is *handicapped*.

3. A person is not ill just because some part of his body is *malfunctioning* in some way, or is *deformed* or *distorted*. For instance, I may be a hunchback, or my eyes may not work properly, or I may have a broken leg: but in none of these cases am I necessarily ill.

4. A person is not ill *just* because he is *suffering* or *in pain*, even if the pain is caused by some part of his body. I am not necessarily ill while I am being beaten or tortured (even continuously): nor when I have the toothache. A child who has a stomach-ache may be ill (if he has incipient jaundice or dysentery), but may not be (if he has eaten too much for dinner).

5. A person may be ill without knowing or feeling *that* he is ill, and even without feeling pain. He may be asleep, or he may be light-headed and say 'I feel marvellous' even when he has a high temperature.

6. A person is not necessarily ill even if 3. and 4. above are both true: that is, even if part of him is malfunctioning, and he is in pain because of it. One can say 'Oh, I'm not ill, I've just got toothache' or 'my corns hurt' or 'the boil on the back of my neck is giving me trouble'.

7. A person is not necessarily ill just because he is fat or smokes a lot. But he is ill if his fatness seriously affects his heart, of if his smoking gives him bronchitis or cancer.

These points suggest that 'being ill' has to do with the *degree* of malfunction affecting his 'normal' life as a person. (We will take a look at 'normal' later.) Because it is primarily *people* who are ill (1), it has to be a matter of malfunction and not just of deficiency (2): we take people for what they are—strong or weak, midgets or giants—and call them ill only if something *inside* them has gone wrong. If something goes wrong enough to affect a man's normal life, he usually (but not always, see 5) knows he is ill: and usually, but not always (5), he is in some kind of pain or distress. The characteristic or model case of someone being ill is when a person catches a specific disease, which gives him a high temperature and compels him to go to bed: he is malfunctioning (the germs are conducting a war which upsets his normally balanced internal ecology) and in pain, and he knows it. But what makes this a case of illness is the degree of *malfunction*: not the fact that he is compelled to go to bed (he might have been sent there for being naughty), nor the fact that he is in pain (someone might be sticking pins into him), nor the fact that he is consciously distressed and unable to lead a normal life (he might have just witnessed the death of his parents and feel unable to carry on for a time). He is ill because his inability to lead a normal life is *due to* malfunction to a considerable degree.

'Considerable degree' (of malfunction) is not something we can pin down. The notion of a 'normal life', as used here, is relative to our expectations. These expectations can be more or less reasonable; and in practice, perhaps, we tend to raise the level of what is 'normal' as we become increasingly able to improve people in health and other aspects. Thus, a society of Africans, all of whom suffered from beri-beri because of a vitamin deficiency, might regard a person with beri-beri as being able to lead a 'normal' life. Few of us would regard ourselves as ill when we have been bitten by mosquitoes or fleas, even though the itch may distract us from our usual pursuits from time to time. Even a wasp-sting may not make us ill—though we might hesitate a bit over this case. But a snake-bite is something different. Again, there comes a point (somewhere between acquiring a sun-tan and coming out all over in blisters, fainting, etc.) at which sunburn makes us ill: so too with the range extending from simply feeling cold or numb at one end of the scale, to frostbite at the other. This flexibility, or relativity, of the notion of 'being ill' is of great importance for the concept of mental health, and we shall return to it later.

This also becomes obvious if we consider, not just the word 'ill', but other closely-allied words such as 'healthy', 'whole' and 'fit'. 'Illness' leans towards the notion of being in pain: 'I feel ill' and 'I am ill' are very close, though not identical (5). 'I feel unwell', 'I feel bad', 'I don't feel so good' are all related to the idea of conscious distress. On the other hand, the notion of being 'fit', 'whole' or 'healthy' leans more towards the malfunction itself; and in the case of 'fit', we may bring in not only malfunction (3) but even deficiency and handicap (2). A 'fit' person, even a really 'healthy' person, implies a standard of performance or capability that would not be met by, say, a cripple, or a man with a weak heart—that is, a heart which is just rather small or feeble, as opposed to a malfunctioning heart.

It would perhaps be too strong to say outright that 'ill' *never* implies deficiency as opposed to malfunction, or that 'fit', 'whole' and 'healthy' can *always* imply it. But the two concepts are certainly different. This can be illustrated by the kind of words used in the romance languages on the one hand, as opposed to our 'health' or the German 'heil'. Phrases like 'mal de mer', 'ça me fait mal', and 'je suis malade' are more like our own 'ill': whereas 'heil' is reminiscent of 'whole' (not deficient), 'holy', 'heal', and 'health'. Of course this is an illustration rather than an argument: but it may help to clarify the point.

'Fit' and 'healthy', like 'ill', also relate to the concept of normalcy that we have already noticed. But here again, it is impossible to draw a sharp line between the healthy and the unhealthy. To put it paradoxically, we can't say exactly just how healthy you have to be in order to be healthy. It depends what sort of standards you set. Nor is there anything very peculiar about this. How intelligent have you got to be to count as intelligent? How 'first-class' a chap must you be to get a first-class degree?

23

Obviously the answers are relative to particular societies or institutions. A 'backward' boy in a grammar school might count as exceptionally bright in a school for 're-tarded' children; and a person who gets a third-class degree at one university might well have got a first-class degree at another.

How can a man's mind be ill?

The very phrase 'mental health' should perhaps strike us as odd, and would certainly have seemed so to a great many societies in the past. As we have noted already, words like 'mad', 'insane', 'dotty', 'raving' and so on are only too common : but 'mental health' may seem to have the air of a phrase specially invented by psychologists who have borrowed it from medicine—perhaps without fully considering its implications. Plato and others have talked about 'sickness of the soul' or 'a man's mind being ill', but this has usually appeared as an obvious metaphor. More normally one might say 'Are you ill *or* mad?', as if the two were in quite different categories.

If we are sufficiently impressed with the dangers of the pseudo-scientific attitude mentioned in the last chapter, we might feel inclined to ask 'How can a man's *mind* be ill?' We might arrive at this question by the following route. Suppose a man is greatly distressed because he has influenza or lockjaw : he has a high temperature, and is in delirium. We say 'Ah, he's ill : there's something wrong with his bloodstream, the germs have got into it'. If pressed, we can say 'His body isn't working properly'. But now suppose another man who is always drunk, or has a tumour of the brain : he too raves and is delirious. Here too we can point to a physical cause (alcohol or the brain tumour). Why should we say that he is *mentally* ill? Because he raves? But so does the first man with 'flu. In both cases the man's body has gone wrong, and in both cases his mind is affected. Hence we might say 'I can see how a man's body may be ill or unhealthy, but how can his mind be?'

Certainly 'mental health' must not be thought of as a special kind of physical health, due to special physical causes. There is no substantial or important difference between a man who has a tumour in the brain, and one who has a tumour in some other part of his body. It is only if we think of the mind as somehow housed or living in the brain that we shall fall victim to this mistake. A man may be driven mad by (say) constant torture of the rest of his body, just as by something going wrong with his brain cells: and conversely, a man may be made physically ill by something in his brain, just as by torture or germs in his bloodstream. 'Mental health' is not dependent on what sort of causes, in what parts of the body, create the trouble. It is in a category of its own. Hence the importance of the question 'How can a man be ill in his mind?' The phrase 'in his mind' tempts us to the answer 'if there's something wrong in his brain'. But the mind is not a physical object like the brain, weighing so much and occupying so much space.

In fact it is misleading to say that a man is ill 'in his body', just as it is to say he is ill 'in his mind'. We must remember that it is primarily *people* who are ill, not parts of people. It is the *man himself* who is ill: that is, who because of some malfunction cannot lead a normal life. We distinguish between physical and mental illness by the *way in which* he cannot lead a normal life. There are some things that people do which have no necessary connection with their minds: such as running, breathing, swimming, and so on. Other things are activities of the mind: reasoning, loving, fearing, being angry. We can say, if we like, that people do the former things 'with their bodies' and the latter 'with their minds'; but we must not seriously believe that the mind is a part of a person, in the same way that an arm or a leg is part of a person. Although 'mind' is a noun like 'arm' or 'leg', it does not

ECMH—C

stand for a physical object or any other kind of object: it is, rather, a quick or shorthand way of referring to certain activities which men engage in.

So far, then, our conclusions are as follows:

1. To be mentally ill is not just to have something wrong with one's *brain*.
2. A person can be mentally ill from physical causes (drugs, torture, etc.).
3. To say that someone is mentally ill is (partly) to say that, because of some malfunction, he is unable to engage in certain activities in a normal way (e.g. thinking and feeling).

But we must be very careful about this notion of 'activities'. Suppose we have a boy who can't swim because of some bodily disease or infirmity. There is no question here of his being mentally ill. Now suppose another boy who can't swim because he has an irrational fear of the water, or because he thinks that the fish will eat him. He may be mentally ill. Plainly we don't call him mentally ill because he can't engage in the activity of swimming: for the first boy can't swim either. Nor—though we might be tempted to think so—do we call him mentally ill because his inability is the result of 'mental causes', whereas the first boy suffers from 'physical causes'. For there are plenty of cases where terror, or some other kind of unreason, may be induced by drugs, brain surgery or other physical means. It is rather that there is 'activity', if we may call it such, that the second boy can't do: namely, he can't adopt a reasonable attitude to water and fish. He can't 'think straight' or 'feel straight' about them.

There are in fact very few 'mental activities' which can't be upset by 'physical' causes, and very few 'physical activities' that can't be upset by 'mental' causes. This is why we need always to bear in mind that the difference between physical and mental health depends on the *way in which* the *person as a whole* is 'below par' or unable to live normally. To take another example: suppose someone finds difficulty in breathing. This may be (a) because he has asthma or bronchitis, or (b) because he is pathologically anxious or frightened. The latter is a case of mental ill-health: but we can't say this *just* because he finds it hard to breathe. We have to show that his finding it hard to breathe is a *symptom*. His mental ill-health consists in his being irrationally anxious: and this might come out in all sorts of other ways—in his sitting down in a paralysed sort of way, withdrawing, stammering, and so on. It is not *that* he can't breathe, nor that he can't breathe *because* he is anxious, but *that he is anxious*, which makes him mentally ill.

Definitions and symptoms

The point we have just made is valid also for physical health. Suppose a man has 'flu. Then he may have a high temperature, a running nose, and so forth. Now although these are *symptoms* of his illness (so that we can say, in one sense, that he is ill *because* he has these symptoms— that they are signs of illness), they do not *define* it. We recognise that he is ill by these signs, but when we say that he is ill we don't *mean* just that he has a running nose, a temperature, etc. But secondly, we don't just mean either that he has 'flu germs inside him. We mean that he can't carry out his normal activities as a person because of a malfunction, due to the 'flu germs, and testified to by the symptoms which the germs produce.

This is particularly important for the concept of mental health, because it often happens that symptoms—or what are taken as symptoms—are held up as definitions. For example, supposing we said that mental health meant doing a steady job, having a settled home, sticking to one marriage partner, etc. What are the objections to this?

First, 'mental health' certainly doesn't *mean* doing a steady job, having a settled home, etc. Secondly, once we realise that this should not be taken as a definition but rather as a set of guiding signs or symptoms, we should want to know that they were due to the person's own malfunction: perhaps a person simply can't do a steady job because employers are only hiring temporary labour these days, or he can't have a settled home because he hasn't got enough money to pay for it. Thirdly, if these phenomena are due to a malfunction in the man himself (as opposed to his society), is it a *mental* malfunction? Perhaps the only jobs available demand great strength, and he happens to be a midget or a paralytic: he isn't *mentally* ill. Fourthly, is the degree of malfunction sufficient to call him *ill*? This will depend on what we regard as a 'normal life' for a person: how far is changing one's job, residence or spouse symptomatic of an important (as opposed to a trivial) malfunction? One might think it trivial: some people change their clothes or their library books a great deal, and we may call them 'restless' or 'discontented' but not 'ill'.

We will look at some of these points later: here I want only to issue a warning about mistaking what may be, but may also *not* be, a symptom of ill-health for a definition of it. Characteristically, we all of us like quick, easy definitions that seem simple to verify. 'You're tired? Overworked? Ill? Take REVIVO and feel better instantly': 'Nail-biting? Nervous at parties? Bored in your suburban home? Get your mental health straight. Be adjusted! Read "How to Face Up to your Responsibilities and Create a Warm World around You"': 'Has life lost its point? Are you in touch with the universe? Do you need a faith to live by? Join the Neomystics and learn the secret of life'. According to our various prejudices, we too quickly put a piece of behaviour—a 'symptom'—into our favourite category: sickness of body, sickness of mind, sickness of soul. But it is not as easy as that. If one is tired, it may
28

signify only that you have been working hard : it may signify that you have anaemia without knowing it : it may signify that you are depressed or anxious : and one can't tell without making sense of the various categories, and finding out which of them it really fits.

In the case of mental health, this means that we must be particularly careful not only about our own, or our society's, uncritical way of thinking, but also of the 'definitions'—which are really often lists of symptoms—which psychologists put forward. But it is not the psychologist's business to *define* mental health, any more than it is the ordinary doctor's business to define physical health. This is not what one pays doctors for. Doctors can tell you when you are ill, and why you are ill. What illness *is* depends on our concept of 'normality'. To some degree, our notion of 'malfunction' also depends on this concept. In physical health, we are all more or less agreed on what is to count as 'normal' living, and hence we agree about what counts as a '*dis*ease' or a '*mal*function'. But in mental health there is, if not disagreement, at least a great deal of confusion : and this we must now consider.

'Normal'

Arguments about what is 'normal'—and this applies to many other words, like 'natural', 'sensible', 'reasonable' and so on—usually fluctuate between two poles or extremes.

On the one hand, we can talk about *facts*. 'Normal' can mean 'average', 'what most people do', 'what usually goes on', or 'common practice'. In a slightly different way, but still talking about facts, we can speak of 'what most people would like to see', 'what society approves of', 'the *mores* of the group' or 'the values of our neighbours' What most people do, and what most people think ought to be done, are both matters of fact. This is different from what *really* ought to be done.

On the other hand, we can talk about individual choices or preferences. Those who think (rightly) that 'normal' in the above sense has no necessary connection with what is right, or what is 'really' mentally healthy or desirable, may feel inclined to say that there is no such thing as 'normality' apart from this above sense: and hence to say that what's right, or healthy, or desirable are ultimately just a matter of individual choice: 'it's a matter of taste'.

Most people, I would guess, still cling to one or other of these extremes. Some talk as if what was common practice was (somehow) necessarily right or healthy. Others rebel against this, and think that there is no way of judging between individual choices: they might say 'Well, it's right for him' or 'If that's the way he chooses to live, there's no way of saying he's wrong'. (This reminds us of the Ideal Child and the Anti-Child mentioned earlier.) The first group of people may identify themselves with current definitions or creeds about mental health: these may derive from a religion, or from contemporary psychology, or from some picture presented to them by state authorities. The second group simply react against this, and leave it to the individual.

I think these two viewpoints have only to be stated to be seen as unreasonable. Indeed, 'unreasonable' is a word of crucial importance here: for it is just this notion of reason that both viewpoints omit. In the context of mental health, the omission is particularly striking. For one of the ways, perhaps the most important way, in which we characterise madness or extreme cases of mental ill-health is by saying things like 'he has lost his reason', 'he lives in a world *of his own*', or 'it's no good arguing with him, he's crazy'. The way in which a mentally unhealthy person fails to 'live normally' is centrally connected with the idea of irrational thought and behaviour. Lunatics who think that they are Napoleon, paranoics who suppose everyone to be persecuting them, people who attack others as if they were enemies when in fact they are quite harmless, and so forth, can all be seen as cases of irrationality.

Hence, although the second viewpoint expressed above is right, inasmuch as what is healthy or desirable is in some sense ultimately dependent on what the individual chooses for himself, such choices can be reasonable or unreasonable, sensible or silly, well-founded or arbitrary. These words—'reasonable', 'sensible', 'well-founded' and so on—do not have to stand for any *particular* set of values or *mores* which some particular society or authority practises or advocates (as the first viewpoint suggests). They rather represent notions which any human being must subscribe to if he is to remain human. 'Mad' does not mean just what a particular society thinks to be mad. The man who thinks he is Napoleon is mad, not just because society thinks him to be wrong, but because he *is* wrong. The man who contradicts himself and talks so wildly that one can hardly communicate with him at all really *is* unreasonable.

It is beyond the scope of this book to give anything like a full justification or explanation of the notion of 'rationality'. But I think we can see dimly that there are certain things which mark out, or perhaps even define, what it is to be a human being (as opposed to a walking biped). Chief among these is the use of *concepts* or *language*. With this goes the notion of using language correctly to describe the world—that is, using it according to the public rules which are essential to any language, and marrying up the words and descriptions of the public language to what we observe in the outside world. This includes what we might call 'facing facts': an 'unreasonable' person, amongst other things, refuses to face facts. Again, the reasonable person acts purposively, 'for a reason' (as we say): he does not just find himself being pushed around by impulses: he is able to communicate with his fellows: he sees the world for what it is, and not just as he would like to see it: and, in general, he is able to *relate* to other people in the world by various kinds of communication—

by using words and otherwise acting intelligently towards them.

To the extent that he cannot 'live normally'—that is, live as a human being—in this way, we call him 'mentally ill' (if his inability is due to a malfunction). His 'abnormality' may take various forms, of course. He may be totally withdrawn and unable to communicate (like autistic children): he may be 'maladjusted' and unable to relate to his fellow-men in a reasonable, fact-facing way: he may find himself compelled by his own feelings, so that his feelings do not go along with his reason: he may have a sudden 'breakdown', so that his rational faculties temporarily disappear: and so on. In all these cases he will, as it were, have resigned his humanity and behave more like an animal, or a machine, or a very young child.

We need to note two important points here. First, we must of course be very careful to make sure that 'normality' only includes those things which every man as such must have, and careful not to sneak in the standards of a society (or of our own prejudices) dressed up as what is necessary for any human individual. It is possible—indeed it often happens—that whole groups or societies are unreasonable, abnormal or mentally ill (consider Nazi Germany). Very often it will be found that we do not know the answer. No doubt we can show, by universally-accepted criteria of rationality, that Aryan blood is not superior, that Jews are not all malicious, etc.: but what do we say about people who believe in God? In angels? In devils, fairies, or table-tapping spirits? In the influence of the stars? In 'the destiny of Communism' or 'the spirit of the German race'? In the wickedness of certain types of sexual activity? In many or all of these cases we have *first* to examine the actual beliefs—to see what they mean, and how the believers would support them—and only *then* to say whether they suggest a believer's inability to be 'normal' or rational. In this examination, it is not so much the truth of the belief which is important, as the

32

way in which he arrives at and supports his belief. The reasonable or sane man is not he who always thinks what is correct: it is he who uses the methods of reason and fact-facing, rather than prejudice, fear, desire or some irrational method, to reach his conclusions. You can be unreasonable but (accidentally) right, and reasonable but (unluckily) wrong.

Secondly, being reasonable or mentally healthy is plainly a matter of *degree*. Nobody is wholly reasonable, and few people wholly unreasonable—otherwise they would cease to be people in the full sense of the word (children brought up by wolves, who can neither talk nor think nor reason, are not really *people*). In much the same way, the notion of 'living normally' in physical health is relative to some standard of physical ability, which may vary from society to society. Most of us regard it as still 'living normally' if all that is wrong with us is, say, a slight itch (see p. 22). So too with mental health; and we shall pick up this key point in a later section (see pp. 57-63).

Some current concepts in mental health

What we have noticed in the last two sections should enable us to make sense of the words and phrases often used in current writings on 'mental health', or at least to be aware of the different ways in which these words and phrases may be used. It would be impossible to consider all of these; and further, it is very unclear from the writings of (and even from long conversations with) psychologists exactly how they are intended. The best we can do is to try to categorise them under a number of headings, so that at least we shall be on our guard when we come across them.

Definitions or part-definitions, and *Symptoms*. We have already noted these two categories in a previous section, but there are a great many words and phrases which might

33

belong to either category. Some words, like 'disturbed', 'un-balanced', 'integrated', 'reality-orientated', 'having a strong ego' and so forth, look like part of what it *means* to describe someone as 'normal' or 'abnormal' (in the sense mentioned in the last section), as 'mentally un-healthy' or 'healthy'. Others, such as 'autistic', 'compulsive', 'depressive', may seem to refer to overt behaviour, or signs, or symptoms *of* ill-health. The parallels in physical health would be (a) words like 'sick' or 'diseased': (b) words and phrases like 'having a high temperature', 'with a blotchy skin', 'with twitching muscles', etc.

Causes of illness. Some words, like 'deprived', seem to refer to the causes of the mental illness. Thus, because it has been fairly well established that children who are deprived of their mothers for long periods when they are young become mentally ill, we can talk of the 'deprived' child. Here we are not talking about symptoms but causes. A parallel from physical health would be something like 'vitamin-starved', or 'germ-infected'.

Types of illness. Very close to causes of illness, above, and often indistinguishable from it, are words used to denote types of mental illness, such as 'psychotic', 'manic', 'neurotic', 'schizophrenic', etc. This is parallel to words and phrases such as 'epileptic', 'cancerous', 'anaemic', 'diabetic' and so on. These are also hard to distinguish from *symptoms*. A 'compulsion neurotic' may refer to a type of illness, but it may also just be a way of talking about overt symptoms, as the word 'compulsive' in *symptoms*, above. But there is a theoretical distinction at least. It is one thing to mention simply what a person does, e.g. wash his hands every half-hour, or touch every lamp-post in the street: another thing to talk of the causes of this piece of irrationality (perhaps some event in early childhood); and yet another to classify this as a 'mental disease', in the general category of 'compulsion neuroses'. The practical difficulties

34

of distinguishing these arise partly from our sheer ignorance about the facts of mental health—our uncertainty about causes and classifications. But we need not go into this here.

Very different from these four ways in which words relating to mental health can be used are three other ways:

Social non-conformity. A word like 'adjusted' can, of course, be used as a part-definition of mental health. The rational or sane man is plainly 'adjusted' in one sense: that is, to put it rather grandly, he is 'adjusted to reality', or 'adjusted to the standards that define what it is to be reasonable'. He is not 'in pieces' or 'disharmonious' but 'integrated'. But 'adjusted' involves a metaphor borrowed from physical objects. Things are adjusted to fulfil particular functions which may have no real connection with mental health. You adjust the height of the blades in an electric razor, adjust your watch to Greenwich Mean Time, 'adjust your dress before leaving' a public lavatory. All these include, of course, the idea of a norm or standard: to that extent adjustment always involves the idea of rationality, of following a rule or fulfilling a purposive function. Even adjusting flowers in a vase suggests some aesthetic ideal of arrangement. But there is nothing in the concept of adjustment itself which implies norms that are incumbent on every healthy human being.

Thus 'adjustment' comes to be used, very often, to refer to some kind of conformity: conformity to a class of children, to the teacher's wishes, to the demands of the neighbours, to the general *mores* of society. It may be right or wrong, healthy or unhealthy, for people to adjust in this sense on particular occasions. Many other words— 'mature', 'responsible', 'adult', 'well-mannered', 'a good mixer'—are equally treacherous. Gipsies are not 'adjusted' to a modern urban civilisation: artists who leave their families and go off to the South Seas are not 'responsible': those who prefer a Bohemian or playboy life, instead of settling down to a wife and children, a bijou suburban residence and a 9-5 job, may (if we like) be called not 'adult'. But what we really want to know, insofar as we are concerned with mental health, is whether we are simply noting their non-conformity to a certain set of social *mores*, or whether (to put it one way) they are *really* maladjusted, irresponsible, immature and so on : that is, whether they are so as human beings rather than as citizens, fathers of families, workers, etc. Of course it may very often be true that those who fail to fulfil their expected social roles are also mentally unhealthy : but it may not be true. (Remember Nazi Germany again.) Schools for 'maladjusted children' are only concerned with mental health insofar as the children are maladjusted as *people*.

Degrees of mental health. Next, we must note a number of words which carry an implication of a certain degree of health or illness. We have already noticed (p. 23) that the word 'ill' carries stronger implications than such words as 'healthy', 'fit', or 'whole', in the case of physical health. 'Mentally ill' is a stronger phrase also, and there are people we would hesitate to call mentally *ill*, though we might not want to say that their mental health was all it should be : indeed, we might refuse to call them mentally *healthy*. A person, for instance, who has undue fears or anxieties about the opposite sex is plainly irrational in an important way. But such a person might lead quite a happy life, for instance in an Oxford college, where he does not come into close contact with women : it would be odd to call him mentally ill, although the distinction may seem a fine one. 'Illness' is much more tied to current notions of what is socially acceptable as 'living normally'.

Even the concept of mental illness, however, is more flexible than we may have suggested. Thus there is a type of person commonly labelled 'the adjusted psychopath', who (let us say) 'lives normally'—usually in a fairly rigid environment such as the army—until he is forty or fifty, but who when he loses the support of this environment immediately behaves in a wildly irrational manner. (Perhaps he steals, defrauds, 'interferes with' girls and so on.) Now looking at the man when he is thirty, in his environment (where he may be very successful and happy), it would be odd to call him 'mentally ill'. But it is even more odd, I think, to say that he has been mentally healthy up to the age of fifty, and then suddenly becomes mentally ill when he leaves his environment. It seems more reasonable to say that he always was mentally ill, but that his symptoms were not easily visible in his earlier environment.

In this way we are led to consider the notion of a 'normal' environment, along with the notion of 'normal' (i.e. rational) living. We might ask 'What sorts of environment can the truly rational man be expected to put up with? Are there environments which would drive anyone mad? If certain children can't conform to existing schools, must there be something wrong with the children—are existing schools the sort of environment that a normal child could tolerate?' These questions again can only be answered by a detailed consideration of the facts. In assessing the degree of mental health, we must take the person's current environment into account. This is important when we consider all words that imply degrees of mental health.

Some such words, like 'mad', 'lunatic', 'insane' (together with the slang synonyms we noted earlier, such as 'round the bend', 'nutty', 'batty', etc.), are very strong. They derive from the picture of a 'raving madman'—someone who has totally lost their reason, like Ophelia in *Hamlet*. Psychologists tell us, with some plausibility, that we are frightened of madness in ourselves, and like to have a scheme which divides the 'mad' from the 'sane' in this very sharp way. Words for 'mentally unhealthy' of a less forceful kind are remarkably rare: 'neurotic' has crept in as a popular term: 'odd', 'queer' (particularly with reference to homosexuals) and others are sometimes used with this implication: and very often we revert to the pseudo-scientific picture mentioned earlier and say that someone 'has a phobia' or 'has a complex' about something. But often we stick to ordinary words like 'sensible' or 'reasonable': and this is perhaps to be preferred, since their meaning is clearer.

Mental deficiency. Finally, there are a number of words which do not really refer to mental health in a strict sense at all. Earlier on (pp. 21-2) we tied the notion of illness to malfunction, as opposed to mere deficiency or weakness. When we speak of 'backward' or 'retarded' children, for instance, there is no necessary reason why we should think there is any malfunction involved. It may be just that the children are slow or stupid; and we do not call the slow-thinking mentally ill, any more than we call a man physically ill just because he cannot run a mile in under four minutes. Of course, it may be that the cause of a child's being backward or 'retarded' is some genuine malfunction: perhaps, for instance, he is pathologically frightened of all teachers, and so has not learnt to read. In the same way, a man may not be able to run the mile in four minutes (or even ten minutes) because he has 'flu. But in that case, words like 'retarded' or 'slow-moving' are being used as descriptions of *symptoms*.

Of course, if they *are* symptoms, then the children are mentally ill. But they are not mentally ill just because they are 'retarded'. The same goes for words like 'mentally deficient', 'moronic', 'handicapped' and many others. There are mental dwarfs and mental giants, mental cripples and mental Olympic hurdlers. We might perhaps not want to call the dwarfs and cripples 'healthy', but we must preserve the distinction between inability due to a deficiency and that due to a malfunction. What we *call* 'stupidity' may, indeed, be symptomatic of a malfunction in many cases: but once we realise this, we naturally say 'This child isn't really stupid, he's just frightened' (or anxious, or depressed, or whatever). There is a genuine category of stupidity or mental incompetence which has nothing to do with ill-ness. Plainly people are not mentally ill because they can-not grasp the theory of relativity, or even if they cannot grasp basic points of Latin grammar.

In much the same way, many psychologists have stressed the idea of 'growth' or 'development'[1]; but it is not clear that this has any necessary connection with mental health —it is not a definition of it, and may not even be sympto-matic of it. A plant can stop growing but still be healthy. In the same way a man may not develop his mind by learn-ing more and more or becoming more 'educated' (in one sense of the word), and yet still remain perfectly healthy. We cannot all be mental giants, either in the sense (men-tioned above) of being super-intelligent, nor in the present sense of being very well-informed or 'educated' : but we are not therefore all ill. It would have to be shown that we were all cases of 'arrested development', if we are to estab-lish any close connection between 'growth' and mental health. As we shall see later (see pp. 57-63), this is by no means an absurd view : but it is not one we can take for granted.

Mad or bad?

We have done something to distinguish the concept of mental health from other concepts, notably from the idea of deficiency, and stressed the notion of malfunction. But there is another category of talk with which talk of mental health is in practice often confused : the category of *moral blame* (vice, wickedness, naughtiness, etc.), which plainly contrasts with the notion of being *ill*. We frequently have to choose between these two categories of talk when decid-ing what to do about criminals, children who break rules, juvenile delinquents and so forth : indeed the problem is a

[1] (For a criticism of this notion, see Peters, 1964.)

very topical one. We cannot say much about this problem here, if only because it raises some very profound and still unsolved philosophical problems in its turn; but it is worth a brief glance.

We blame a person (or feel justified in calling him 'wicked', 'immoral', etc.), not when there is something wrong *with him*, but when *he does* something wrong. To be blameworthy or praiseworthy, he has to do it 'of his own free will', and not under compulsion or threats: it has to be *his fault*: it has to be true that he could have done something else instead, that he could have acted otherwise. Very roughly, we reserve praise and blame for those situations in which a man knows what he is doing, and where nothing prevents him from acting otherwise. We begin to praise and blame children as people (rather than just patting them or frowning at them as at animals) when they have developed some degree of rationality: the mastery of language and concepts, the ability to form intentions and to act for reasons.

Very roughly again, praise and blame are our reactions to situations in which we treat people as rational (and hence as moral) beings, who know what they are doing, know what the rules are, and have a choice of alternatives. It is, briefly, for their *intentions*—and perhaps to some extent for their ability to carry out their intentions if there is no undue external pressure—that we praise and blame them. A man's intentions and choices are not *part* of him in the same way that his arms or legs are part of him: they *are* him. We react to the man himself: we do not and cannot react to him as to a 'mental case' or to someone under compulsion. For to be under compulsion, in general, is to have one's intentions or decisions thwarted or thrust on one by an outside force. And this is very different from having the wrong intentions or making immoral decisions.

The reader is advised to pursue these points elsewhere[2]:

[2] (See Peters, 1966, chapter X, and the references to other works there mentioned.)

but from this very brief discussion a number of considerations arise which are highly relevant to mental health.

The application of moral judgements, and the initiation of the child into a form of life in which he is treated (and learns to behave) as a rational, free being, are inseparable. Rationality—and to some extent mental health—depends, therefore, on maintaining the notion of moral rules (and the praise and blame that goes with them): it will not do to treat children who are genuinely bad or naughty as if they were mad or mentally ill. It would be fatal for their development as rational beings.

To retain the notions of praise and blame, and also of reward and penalties, does not commit us to any kind of vindictive or cruel moralising, or treatment of the sort that it is still fashionable to associate with the Victorian Age. If a child consciously and deliberately breaks an agreed rule or contract (by lying, stealing, cheating, etc.), then he is to blame: to use a useful if old-fashioned metaphor, he is not 'playing the game', and it is no use pretending that he is. He has, as it were, let us down as a rational, rule-following being. It follows that, insofar as he is cheating, he cannot be regarded in the same light as we regard any other non-cheating player, and he must be dealt with by some method or other. But it does not follow that he has to be beaten, spoken to severely, put in the corner or sent to bed without supper.

Nor does it follow—and this is very important, as we shall see later (pp. 53-7) that there is not something wrong *with him*, as well as its being *his fault*. A man may act freely and in full knowledge of what he is doing and how it relates to rules (of law, of the school, of morality), so that he is certainly 'responsible' and may if he does wrong be classed as 'immoral' or 'wicked'. But this is not to say that his behaviour was magical or unpredictable—a kind of sudden twitch for which he is somehow still responsible: indeed, if his behaviour were like that, totally random, we should not call *him* responsible. No doubt there are causes, which psychologists or others could in principle trace, of why he acted so. Even if his action was carefully thought out, and could be explained by reference to his conscious motives and intentions, no doubt there are causes which could explain why he had those motives and intentions at that time, why he chose as he did. We may say, if we like, that those causes represent something wrong *with him*: and say this is not to deny that his particular action was *his fault*. Wickedness can always be a symptom of mental ill-health: but this is not to say that the two categories can be merged in theory, or should be merged in practice.

It is, therefore, not only possible, but in many cases necessary, for the teacher to use both categories: to use the roles, one might say, of both judge and therapist. A child is deliberately naughty, and requires judgement. There is perhaps an underlying reason or cause, of a 'mental health' kind, why he is naughty: and this may require therapy. What sort of therapy must depend on our view of the causes. Although (see above) we are not committed to treating him in some unpleasant way, we are not committed to treating him in a pleasant way either: it may be a very good form of treatment to slap him, or send him to bed. Not all cases of bad behaviour are due to lack of love: some may be due to an insufficiently-developed awareness of the real world and how people in the real world expect things from one—and a sharp reminder of this may well be psychologically beneficial.

4
One aspect of mental health

In the Introduction it was suggested that 'mental health' was something important, not only for experts but for every individual: and also that it was something which, in a sense, individuals could only acquire for themselves or be helped to acquire—not something which could be handed to them on a plate. This is, however, true only of one aspect of mental health. It is a crucially important aspect, and the one which is of greatest concern to teachers and education in general: and we must begin by making clear what aspect we are talking about.

Exercise and learning

Let us start with a parallel from physical health. A great deal of physical health obviously depends on things which other people can do for us. They can give us the right food, air, sunlight, and so on: they can avoid doing things to us which cause a malfunction, such as tying wires tightly round our skulls (as some Africans do), or giving us poison: and if, despite their efforts, we fall ill, they can give us drugs, operate on us, and so forth. But there are a number of things they cannot do for us, and which we have to do ourselves. They cannot walk for us, or swim for us, breathe for us, or take exercise for us.

This is not because medical science has not advanced sufficiently: it is because these are things which we must, logically, do for ourselves. Somebody can push my legs, but that is not *me walking*. Now a great many cases in physical health depend precisely on the individual doing things for himself in this way. In physiotherapy, for instance, although the therapist can do a great deal for the patient, part of his job is to get the patient himself to do various exercises—to lift his stiff leg, wiggle his partially paralysed fingers and so on. In physical education children are encouraged to learn things which will help to keep them healthy : and not only facts about hygiene, but how to use their bodies in particular ways.

The position is essentially similar with mental health : though, as I shall argue, we need to place more stress on things that an individual can only do for himself than in the case of physical health. We have seen (p. 24) that mental health can be caused by a great many things : malfunction can be induced by drugs, or other straightforward 'physical' causes. These we may leave to those scientists who specialise in the brain, in glandular development, chemistry and so forth. Again, pressures of environment may easily drive a man mad : constant torture, brutal interrogation and 'brainwashing', and many other things. (Cutting off sensations, and hence points of reference, by suspending a person in glycerine is alleged to induce temporary insanity by disorientating him.) These again we can leave on one side. Psychologists will stress all the things that parents can do to promote or diminish mental health in their children : by depriving them, beating them, failing to cuddle or love them, not giving them a firm set of rules, and so forth. Insofar as we are talking here simply about *things given* to children (as to animals), things which may be necessary conditions of developing rationality in the future, like food and air, we may leave these on one side also : not because they are not important, but because they do not come under the aspect of mental health which we want to examine.

In fact, however, psychologists and others are very apt to confuse these latter requirements of mental health with the aspect in which we are interested. It is easy to think of 'love' and 'security', 'affection' and 'deprivation', as

44

things with which we (as it were) feed children, as we feed them with milk; and in some sense, sometimes, we may be right to think of them in this way. Thus some psychologists will talk about the importance of 'stimulation' for a baby: this seems to mean fondling, cuddling, touching, moving its limbs and so on—the sort of thing that could be done by a robot 'child-stimulator', if we cared to invent one. As we said before, insofar as we are talking about establishing the conditions necessary for mental health, all this is quite satisfactory. But we feel uneasily (and rightly) that there are senses of 'love' and 'security' which this kind of talk does not cover.

Loving a child, or making a child 'feel loved', is not like loving a garden. The crucial difference is that children, even when quite young, think and feel, whereas gardens do not. Children conceptualise and use language. A child cannot, in the full sense, 'love' or 'feel loved' unless he knows something of what 'love' means, and can identify cases of it. Nor can he 'feel secure' unless he has some idea of (say) his parents always being there, food not always being dashed from his lips, rules being permanently kept, and so forth. People do not, in the full sense, 'feel loved' or 'feel secure' when they are asleep: they are just asleep. To feel things, in the sense we are talking about, is essentially bound up with *learning* to feel them: that is, with concepts and language.

The behaviour of parents (and teachers), therefore, affects the child as a form of *teaching*, as well as just by way of doling out stimulation or food. To call it 'teaching' is of course misleading, insomuch as parents or teachers do not consciously direct their behaviour with the child in view. Nevertheless, the child does in fact learn to structure his world, as he becomes more and more rational and capable of using and understanding language: and much of the way in which he structures it, and the feelings he attaches to different parts of it, will depend on the way in which adults around him behave. Much also

45

may depend on other factors, such as his own body, the bodies of his parents, and inevitable experiences of his early life. How large a part these other factors may play is an important question (see pp. 62-3).

It is very obvious that some people have done better than others in this very elementary, but crucially important, form of learning : and there is no doubt that a person's attitude to (say) women may be largely dependent on what he has learnt, or picked up, from his mother—even though his mother may not have consciously *taught* him anything about women at all. A great many forms of irrationality are thus the product of what we may call *mislearning*: that is, the product of an early mistake— for instance, in attributing certain feelings to certain people. This is to be sharply distinguished from *ignorance*: it is, rather, to have one's concepts and feelings muddled up, to be irrational and to entertain beliefs which do not accord with the facts.

This distinction can be perceived clearly enough in adults. Some people may be ignorant about Jews: they may even, not unreasonably trusting what some of their friends say, think that they have certain characteristics which they do not have. But this is different from being *prejudiced* against Jews. In the first case, they simply do not know : and the rational man, if he has not enough evidence, will say that he does not know. In the second case, the person does not bother about evidence at all. He just hates Jews, without even knowing why he hates them. Similarly, there are a large number of cases where people have, as it were, been *taught wrong* about (say) negroes: so that they come to associate certain things with negroes that in fact are not necessarily associated with them (dirt, stupidity, sexual precocity, etc.). Here again, this 'teaching' may not really be teaching. The kind of expression a parent wears when talking about negroes, the general attitude of one's neighbours, occasional remarks like 'Ugh, a nigger!' and so forth may cause a

46

person to form his concepts of negroes in an irrational way. Orwell's *1984*, Huxley's *Brave New World* and many other books paint vivid pictures of this kind of irrationality.

If this is a correct account of one aspect of mental health, it is obvious why this aspect is important to every individual. For there is only one way in which a person who is irrational as a result of mislearning can be cured: and that is, by being educated out of it. This conflation of the notions of 'cure' and 'education' will need further justification; but it is not too remote from cases in physical health, in which (for instance) a man who has walked wrongly for years, and thus developed an unhealthy posture, has to be taught to walk properly. If he really has to be taught, no amount of drugs, massage, surgery or mechanical aids will do it for him: he has to learn and practise it himself. In the same way, you cannot altogether *make* or *force* people to be rational or mentally healthy, in the sense which we are talking about: it is a form of mislearning, and though we can give them every aid to learning better, they must ultimately do it themselves.

This aspect of mental health, then, is in my view not dissimilar from the learning (or relearning) of any other material. If a boy has muddled ideas about Latin grammar or mathematics, you cannot improve him by drugs or discipline alone: eventually he must understand for himself what the rules are, and learn to apply them. Simply forcing him to go through the motions might help, but it would never be enough: for however many motions he went through, and however correctly, he would not really know what he was doing, i.e. what rules he was following. It would be like training a dog to write a 4 in the sand whenever the trainer wrote $2 + 2$: the dog would not really be *adding up*.

But this is very far from proving that the kinds of mislearning or irrationality which we can see in adults, and

47

which we may suspect to have their origins in childhood mislearning, are an important aspect of mental health. For, firstly, they may not cause anything that we could call a malfunction: and secondly, even if they do, the malfunction may not be serious enough to say that many people are 'mentally unhealthy' as a result of it. They may still be able to 'live normally', as we have put it. We must now consider both these points.

Irrationality and the unconscious

That human beings are irrational as opposed to merely ignorant, and that this irrationality is often sufficient to describe them as 'mentally ill', can hardly be denied. What may be questioned, however, is whether the causes or reasons for their irrationality are often of the kind I have described: that is, due to mislearning. For there are, of course, plenty of other available causes: it may be their glands, or their brain cells, or the weather. In particular it may be questioned whether Freud and others have been right in attributing the causes or reasons of this irrationality to experiences in early childhood. To raise these questions, I fear, is to bring in the whole notion of the unconscious mind: and whilst a brief consideration of this is important, I must again advise the reader to pursue the subject elsewhere.[1]

If we begin by ridding our minds of what Freud either said or is thought to have said, it is in fact very difficult to resist the belief that many types of irrationality are due to mislearning, and can be remedied by a process which has as much right to be called 'educating' as to be called 'curing'. Consider first the kind of world-picture which was held by most ancient civilisations, in which they, their country, and their world were the centre of the universe: in which their gods were men and women like them, only perhaps more powerful and immortal: and in which they

[1] Peters, 1960 and MacIntyre, 1958.

themselves were 'civilised' and the others 'barbarians': in which certain objects or activities had magical powers or were taboo: in which prayers, or virtue, made the crops grow. Now this picture is not simply the result of ignorance: if anything, it is the cause of ignorance, in that if they had been willing to abandon it they might have made more progress with science and other rational activities. If they were merely ignorant, they might have said, 'Well, we just don't know the answer to lots of these questions'. But in fact they had *reasons*—though bad reasons—for having this picture: amongst other things, it helped to sustain their own sense of security and importance in a bleak universe, where they were surrounded by problems which they did not know the answer to.

In cases of this kind, we must not imagine the human mind to be a blank sheet of paper, a *tabula rasa*, which is occasionally pushed around by the malfunctioning of glands, brain cells, and so on. The mind takes on a shape, or builds up a conceptual scheme to which feelings are attached, which welcomes the acceptance of some truths and rejects others as unwelcome, too terrifying to be entertained. The process is like being hypnotised or brainwashed by another person, rather than like being fed with false information or being ignorant. Under (and after) hypnosis, a person will have a set of feelings, *and reasons attached to them*, about certain things that the hypnotist wishes to impose upon him. In this case, we say that the person is 'rationalising': that is, although the person supports his outlook—his sudden desire to open the window, for instance—by reasons ('it's got much hotter in here'), these reasons aren't the *real* reasons. He just makes them up, *unconsciously*, to justify what is in fact an obedience to a hypnotic command.

A good deal of what seems to be reasoning is really rationalisation. What makes it so is not that the reasons themselves are necessarily bad: in the case above, where the hypnotist tells the man 'Five minutes after you're out of the trance you'll open the window', it might actually be the case that the room got suddenly hotter, so that the reason 'it's got much hotter in here' would be a good reason. But it would not be *his* reason: that is, it would not be a reason *in virtue of which he was acting*. We could test this by trying the same scene in a room which didn't get any hotter: and if the man acted in the same way, we could plausibly conclude that he had been rationalising in the first case too, even though in that first case his reason happened to fit the facts.

The majority of cases, in our society at least, where people are irrational in this way, concern human beings (rather than physical objects or world-pictures). Think of a man in love with, or infatuated with, a girl whom he sees in quite a false light. 'She makes me so happy', he says. (But we know she doesn't: he trembles at the knees, his face is strained and anxious, he can't sleep: this isn't what we mean by 'happy'. He can be wrong about *his own feelings too*.) 'She is so kind to me, we have so much in common'. (She isn't and they don't: we only have to look with unprejudiced eyes.) Or the boy who says 'I simply despise that silly old headmaster, I'm not frightened of him'. (But he is frightened, and anxious to placate—if he can do it so that nobody notices, not even himself: we can watch him doing it.) Cases could be multiplied.

A number of points need to be made here about this particular kind of unreason.

Such people are not *lying*, in the sense of consciously being deceitful. They are, rather, pretending *to themselves*. Other people may in fact not be deceived at all: we frequently attribute emotions, purposes and intentions to someone which he does not know he has, and we are often right.

A person can be cured/educated out of this sort of irrationality. He can be brought to see what his true feelings are. The boy that says 'I don't want to swim, it's silly' can be brought to see that what he really feels is 'I'd like to swim like all the other boys, but I'm frightened of the water'.

On the other hand, people seem very well defended against admissions of their true feelings: they have a vested interest, one might say, in *not* owning up to them. And if they have reasons for their false picture of their own feelings, or of other people's feelings, or of the facts, then this is not surprising. The boy doesn't want to admit (to himself or anyone else) that he is frightened, because it makes him feel small and cowardly, which he doesn't like.

The process of getting them to lower these defences, to 'own up', seems to be partly a matter of persuading them in the course of conversation to see things for what they are ('But look, she isn't really kind to you, think of the time when . . .'): but partly also a matter of creating a context in which they don't feel at all threatened, or in which they don't feel obliged to 'put up a show'. The boy who is scared of the water needs to be able to feel that, if he brings out this feeling, he will not lose too much face.

What we have described here, in a very simple form, is what is supposed to happen in a psychoanalytic or psycho-therapeutic situation. But before we say any more about such situations, and involve ourselves in the whole cluster of feelings and prejudices and myths which attach themselves to notions like 'psychoanalysis', we need to notice one concept in particular which is central to the kind of 'mental ill-health' or irrationality we are consider-ing, and without which the notion of 'the unconscious' would be largely unnecessary. This is the concept of *repression*.

It is crucial to our whole understanding of this aspect of mental health that we do not regard 'repression' along purely physical lines; as if a 'desire' were like water flowing freely, and a 'repressed desire' were like water dammed up. Many people still interpret the post-Freudian picture of the human mind (and it ought to be said at once that Freud himself seems to have been unclear about how it should be interpreted) as if it were a physical, perhaps a hydrodynamic, model of various 'forces' at work 'in' the 'id', the 'unconscious', and so forth. But in fact nearly all the words used in this picture are words normally used to describe what human beings *do*, and not just a series of odd events that *happen* to them. 'Want', 'desire', 'fear', 'hate', 'love', 'guilt', 'anger'—all these imply some kind of consciousness on the part of a person, and some ability to conceptualise and use language. The explanation offered for the cases of irrationality we are considering, therefore, is not that such people are sufferers from minor or major break-downs of rationality due to a number of unfortunate events which are in no way 'their fault'. It is not like being made irrational by drugs, malfunctioning glands, or what-ever. It is—partly, at least, and on the Freudian view quite understandably—we who cause our own irrationality.

Now when we see people behaving irrationally about other people, we often feel tempted to summarise their behaviour by saying 'What he really wants, though he doesn't know it, is such-and-such' or 'It's as if he really intended to do so-and-so'. On our view, this does not simply mean that he behaves in a certain way, i.e. the way in which a man who did have certain wants or intentions would behave. Nor can it mean that the person is con-sciously saying to himself at the time 'I want this' or 'I intend to do that'. It means that the person *unconsciously* wants or intends something: and this would be wholly mysterious unless we had a picture of human beings, in terms of which they can have wants and intentions *and then repress them*—to such a degree, indeed, that they may forget that they ever had them, and be unable to remem-ber except under certain special circumstances (as in psychoanalysis).

In fact this is a very common human experience. We frequently formulate wants or intentions, and then forget them under the pressure of events. Very often we have an obvious vested interest in doing so. During quarrels with his wife, a man may well want to hurt her or even, temporarily, to kill her : certainly to humiliate her. At the time he can be quite conscious of this. But afterwards, if he is the sort of man who finds it hard to live with such feelings within a marriage, he may easily deny to himself that he ever wanted or intended anything of the kind. 'We have our rows occasionally, but of course I love her—no, I never want to hurt her or humiliate her.' Again, examples could be multiplied.

It may help to clarify this general point if we say that the theory which lies behind the notion of the unconscious is, as it were, a *historical* theory, and not primarily a *scientific* one. The story told by Freud and other psychologists of the unconscious is not primarily a story of what has *happened* to a person but a story of what the person *did* and *felt*. The same is true of ordinary history. Though writers of history may mention certain facts, such as that the inhabitants of a city were killed in an earthquake, they are chiefly interested in the intentions, purposes and feelings of past human beings. 'Why did Brutus kill Caesar?' is not a demand for some scientific law of which Brutus is an instance : it is a demand for his intentions, what he said to himself at the time. The best type of verification we could imagine for it would be Brutus' private diary : just as the best type of verification we can get for the Freudian story is the admissions of individuals about their past intentions.

The post-Freudian picture

In looking rather more closely at this general picture, we do not at all need to get involved with the detailed theories of Freud or any other psychologist. *Particular* stories about the repressed desires and intentions of human beings may be false : our interest is to see the possibility of telling such a story at all. And, obviously, what makes the telling of such a story plausible is the conditions of childhood, during which the individual is alleged to undergo a number of crucial repressions, denials, changes or transferences of feeling from one object or person to another, and so forth. This plausibility is three-fold:

(a) Although children can conceptualise and are to some degree rational, they have not such a firm grasp on reality, or on the appropriate concepts, as adults have: to gain such a grasp takes time, experience and a good deal of linguistic sophistication.

(b) What we described earlier as 'the pressure of events' is infinitely stronger for children than for most adults. Children are weak, dependent for their security on adults, and have to deal with very strong feelings without having the proper equipment.

(c) Because of (a) and (b), there is—to put it baldly—much more likelihood of children 'making mistakes', or falling victim to the kind of self-generated irrationality we are concerned with. It is correct to call it 'self-generated', since they do actually make the mistakes themselves: but this is not to say that these mistakes are not natural and inevitable to the situation—we could hardly expect anything else. (This point we shall take up later.) Mistakes made during a formative period, however, are likely (as every teacher of any subject knows) to be more important than later errors: and hence the persistence of these errors, so that they distort our perceptions and beliefs as adults, should not surprise us.

We must observe at this point that the post-Freudian picture is not solely a historical explanation of the individual's *mistakes*, though these are naturally most apt to attract our attention when we think in terms of mental health. It is, rather, an attempt to give the basic history of every individual, including what we call his 'normal' life as well as his abnormal'. For example—and it does not matter here whether this particular story is right or wrong—the kind of historical sketch Freud gives of the sexual desires and 'love-objects' of a boy-child helps to explain adult heterosexuality as well as adult homosexuality. It explains why men find women attractive (briefly, because they identify women in adult life with their mothers on whom their first desires were naturally centred), as well as why some men fail to find women attractive (perhaps because their fathers were more affectionate than their mothers, perhaps because they were frightened of the extent of their desire for their mothers).

Moreover, it must be noted that the picture also includes a great deal that can more naturally be interpreted as science than as history: that is, it concerns *causes* which *affect* the child as well as *reasons* which the child *has*. Exactly which parts of the picture fit which interpretation best is not our concern here. Even in adults, it is often very hard to distinguish the two in practice: and it is even harder in the case-history of the child, where the distinction between conscious and unconscious processes is less sharp. Thus, insofar as there are cases of 'repression' which are themselves unconscious—i.e. where the child does not entertain a feeling consciously and then represses it—the picture is irrelevant to our present concern. My own view is that far more of the picture is concerned with what was conscious, but has become unconscious, than some writers suppose. Whether this is correct does not matter here.

What matters far more is the general effect this picture must have on our attitude towards and understanding of human beings. Here too we must beware of seeing Freud as 'a second Copernicus' (even if he saw himself so)—that is, as primarily a scientist. In an important way his skill is more like that of the novelist: to use a high-sounding phrase, we can see him as a sort of universal novelist of human nature. In a way not dissimilar from that in which a great novelist of character—Dostoevsky, for example —gives us a picture of human beings which is more profound, thorough, penetrating, and (one might say) three-dimensional than the flat, superficial, two-dimensional pictures we often make do with, so the post-Freudian understanding of man takes far more into account, and makes more sense of it, than we were able to do before.

We have now the picture of a man with a *history* (if he is regarded as a patient, we say 'a case-history'). The things children do, and the many ways in which adults behave which is connected with their childhood, become intelligible and are no longer disconnected. We have a picture of a man whose present behaviour is very much influenced by his past decisions, intentions and motives. That men are like this we always knew; in a sense Freud merely fills out the picture. We miss the point if we speak of men being influenced 'by their unconscious minds', or 'by the id'; for we shall be tempted to class these pseudo-entities along with other causes, thereby forgetting that, in a vitally important sense our past intentions and desires *are ourselves*. Under psychoanalysis a man is not commiserated with 'because he is suffering from a complex', as it might be from a boil: he is brought to realise that *he* is wrong, not so much that there is something wrong *with him*. It is he who sees the world wrongly, who does not fully comprehend his own emotions and those of other people, whose intentions and purposes are irrational: who, in a word, is mentally ill.

It is worth noting a general distinction, in the two kinds of mental illness with which this aspect of mental health is concerned. There is, first, the psychotic: he is the man whose appreciation of reality is grossly distorted, even for his conscious intellect. He may really think that other people are persecuting him, for instance: or he may invent, say, a kind of God who he believes to be punishing

56

him. The neurotic, secondly, is less disturbed in that he has some awareness of his own irrationality. He knows that there isn't really any point in touching every lamp-post, or that washing his hands fifty times a day is really rather silly: but somehow he doesn't *feel as if* he knows. There is, we might say, a part of him that doesn't believe what his reason believes: but it is better to say that *he himself* doesn't 'really' believe it. These two categories can be roughly distinguished: but of course only roughly, and they are worth mentioning only to display the two sorts of irrationality which may be involved in mental illness of this general kind.

Mental health and the level of 'normality'

The general concept of health was explained earlier in terms of a man's being unable to 'live normally' due to some malfunction: and the notion of 'normality' in regard to mental health in particular was explained as being similar to rationality, since this offers a neutral and acceptable account of what is a 'normal' function for human beings in their 'mental' aspect. We also hinted (p. 33) that the notion of 'normality' was relative: that is, to put it briefly, dependent on where we set our sights. In whole cultures, where everyone is afflicted with a particular disease like beri-beri, it is intelligible to speak of *everyone* not being able to 'live normally', or of everyone being physically ill. Is this possible in the case of mental health?

It is, of course, both logically and practically possible. Logically possible, because 'normal' does not (in this sense) mean 'average', but relates to a norm which is to some extent arbitrary or of our own making. And practically possible, because we do recognise groups and cultures, sometimes even whole countries, which seem to us mentally ill: not only the inhabitants of lunatic asylums, but groups of (say) early religious fanatics, or instances like the Nazi movement. It must be remembered that *in practice*, life being what it is, we tend to avoid saying that most people are abnormal. Since we have to carry on with the institutions and general standards that are current in our society, we tend to set our sights in such a way that only a small proportion of cases count as 'abnormal'. For this there are many reasons, one of which is that it is difficult for us to set ourselves standards which are too high to live up to, and which (because they are so high) seem of little practical value, 'utopian'.

Nevertheless, this reluctance cannot be allowed to dominate our thinking. There have always been those whose picture of human beings was not the form 'most people are more or less all right, but of course there are a few who are physically ill/mentally ill/unduly stupid/ unduly immoral/sinful'. One obvious picture which represents dissatisfaction with this complacent attitude is that of traditional Christianity, at least from St. Augustine onwards. In this picture, the force of which cannot be denied though the form may be unfashionable today, we are *all* 'sinners', 'unprofitable servants', 'spiritually sick'. We are all 'below par'. To use one of its most powerful myths, man is a fallen creature: since the Fall, none of us are 'living normally'. It is as if we were all diseased, all twisted, distorted or perverted: as if we all had rickets, or suffered from a vitamin deficiency. Hence we all need 'saving' (compare 'curing'). It is not the case that we all enter the world, 'trailing clouds of glory' as Wordsworth says: nor is it the case that we are just ignorant animals that need to be taught rather than cured. We are in some way *ill.*

We do not have to believe in the cruder forms of 'original sin' to take the point, which is essentially a point about what some writers call 'the human condition', and which has been made in many different forms and terms (of which Freudian terms are only one instance). Whatever terminology we prefer, however, it is hard for anyone who has considered human nature deeply to dismiss the point as absurd. Such facile and sunny optimism is not found in great works of art and literature, any more than we find much of it in real life. Nor are we committed to a universal pessimism, to the view that everybody is hopelessly ill all the time, that nothing ever comes right, that there is no such thing as love or reason. We are only committed to the view that most or all human beings are substantially below par in their mental health.

For the aspect of mental health with which we are concerned, this view seems to me very plausible indeed. Insofar as mental maladies are the product of unusual physical causes, such as an excess of thyroid, it would be absurd to hold such a view. But insofar as they are the product of the childhood situation, it gains a good deal of plausibility both from common-sense considerations about the intrinsic difficulties of that situation (see pp. 53-4), and from the specific observations of psychologists. It involves the recognition that children mislearn a great deal, and that this mislearning is not always, not even usually, adequately remedied before or after they become adults. This mislearning results in phenomena to which we are well accustomed, but which to describe as 'normal' in the present context would be to take a very superficial view : such things as sexual dissatisfaction, status-seeking, depression, bad-temper, pathological anxiety, an irrational attitude to money, the inability to love, cruelty and racial prejudice. If these are not enough for us, let us consider the phenomenon of mass killing, whether in the form of 'death on the roads' or in the form of war, and ask ourselves whether this is the result merely of sheer ignorance, rather than of a very deep form of mislearning.

The post-Freudian picture also suggests to us a second point, which may serve further to demolish the view that 'mental health' is the rule rather than the exception. By picturing the individual, not just as an isolated and narrow consciousness at a particular point in time, but as compounded of his past wishes, intentions and motives[2] in the way we have described, we inevitably judge differently not only about how 'normal' a person is, but about what constitutes the person himself. It is now no longer possible for a person totally to disown his past history, since we can see the way in which that history continues to influence our actions and feelings. Even things like dreams and slips of the tongue (if Freud is to be believed), are not just things that happen to us: they are essentially connected with what we are, what we want, or what we fear. This is not to say that such things are, in a strictly moral sense, 'our fault': but they are not mere misfortunes either.

This means that our judgements on the rationality or irrationality of individuals must take into account the degree of consciousness (we might say, the extent of the ego) which an individual has achieved, as well as the degree of rationality that he consciously displays. We might imagine a well-integrated and harmonious person, whose personality was yet very narrow: who disowned or cut himself off from various feelings, as a man might cut himself off from the sexual life by self-castration. For what he is, such a man might behave quite rationally. But we would feel that he has purchased his rationality at the price of losing some of his humanity: or, to put it another way, that he is cheating. The whole point of rationality is to deal with the elements of life as we have them, including our own feelings. Lying behind our notion of 'a man being able to live normally', therefore, is a picture not only of what counts as 'living normally', but also of what counts

[2] (The exact status of Freud's own theories is uncertain. Some claim him to have been talking essentially about *wishes* (see R. S. Peters, 1965). My own view is that there is no one central theory in Freud, and that various strands in his thought occupy different logical positions. At least one of these strands, in my view, is concerned with the possibility of human beings engaging unconsciously in activities which entail rule-following and the use of language (e.g. intentions, beliefs, purposes, etc.). Much remains to be discussed here: but see also Peters, 1960.)

as 'a man'. And although this second question is very difficult to determine, there would come a point at which we would say that someone was malfunctioning as a person because he is no longer a person in the full sense.

We have here side-stepped a number of very difficult problems, which we cannot solve in this context. In practice, however, it nearly always happens that a consciousness that is insufficiently 'full' is also liable to be in conflict and easily overthrown: that a person who disowns important parts of his personality is liable to find that they will take their revenge in some way or other. The notion of 'a strong ego', often held up as a central feature of mental health (and perhaps a definition of it), includes the idea of *extent* as well as integration: just as the notion of 'a strong country' in politics includes the idea of a large and hence powerful country, as well as of a well-integrated country, not torn by civil war. (Indeed the parallel between countries and individuals has been profitably pursued by some modern psychoanalysts, notably R. E. Money-Kyrle.)

A third point is also relevant here. We have spoken before (see pp. 21-3) of both physical and mental illness as a form or result of malfunction rather than of mere deficiency, and throughout this Part of the book we have been contrasting irrationality (malfunction) with mere ignorance (deficiency). But, as we have also noted (p. 33), the somewhat wider notion of 'health' or 'fitness' makes it difficult in practice to maintain a strict dividing line. This is particularly true of mental health, in that aspect of it with which we are now concerned. For unless a child is, so to speak, 'fed' with appropriate concepts and objects for his feelings, he is virtually bound to display unreason as well as sheer ignorance. There is no reason why anyone should think anything in particular about, say, nuclear physics or Latin grammar: one can here be merely ignorant or 'uneducated' without being irrational. But in more emotional matters, in the way the child sees other people and himself, there are strong pressures on him to formulate some kind of view: and unless he is given what we might call a good 'basic education', a sound upbringing, his views will inevitably be 'primitive' in the sense which implies irrationality as well as being just badly-informed.

To put it another way: whilst we must preserve the distinction between 'curing' and 'educating' (in that those who are merely stupid or misinformed do not need to be *cured*, nevertheless a deficiency may result in malfunction —just as a vitamin deficiency may cause physical ill-health. One such deficiency may be the result of a failure to create conditions for the child under which he may learn the first steps of rationality: perhaps, conditions under which he will acquire a proper grasp of *language*. If there is such a deficiency, malfunction will certainly follow.

In actual cases, the different types and causes of mental illness may often be multiple. It may be, for example, that (a) some purely physical cause predisposes a child in such a way that he finds it hard to relate properly to the outside world: (b) partly because of this, he fails to pick up the basic tools of such relationship (including a proper use of language) which may be offered to him in his upbringing: (c) because of this, he becomes a prey to irrational fears, outbursts of aggression, etc., and maintains only a precarious consciousness which is constantly threatened by unconscious factors. Some autistic children may perhaps fit this example: but it is difficult to categorise cases along the lines of the conceptual distinctions we have drawn until more facts are known about the cases themselves.

The above is, of course, grossly over-simplified as an account of one particular aspect of mental health. But though its precision and accuracy may be challenged at many points by both philosophers and psychologists, I think we have said enough to be clear about the general importance of this aspect for education. This importance rests on two general beliefs.

There is a kind of mental ill-health of which the individual cannot be miraculously cured by experts, but of which he must in an important sense cure himself (although of course he may be helped). He must *relearn* what he has *mislearned*.

This kind of mental ill-health is extremely common, and perhaps universal. For the picture suggested to us is one of universal human mislearning. We have come to accept some degree of mislearning as a norm, but this is a short-sighted and superficial view.

If this is so, it follows that teachers cannot regard their pupils as (for the most part) mentally healthy. It does not, of course, necessarily follow that it is the teacher's job to improve their mental health. It might be thought that the job should be left to other people : or that the teacher's prime concern was to 'educate' the children in the narrower sense of teaching them subjects, so that he would only spend such time as he had left over on 'mental health'. I do not myself think that either of these views is very plausible. We shall consider in the final Part of this book just how this aspect of mental health relates to the teacher's role : but we have spent some time on elucidating this aspect, just because these questions depend very much on how seriously we take the picture I have presented. Thus, those who suppose that 'everyone is really more or less all right', and that the kinds of irrationality stressed by certain psychologists are much overrated, will no doubt take the whole thing as a kind of false alarm. I can only advise such people to read the relevant literature and to keep their eyes open. Ultimately there is no cut-and-dried proof : it is always possible not to see the merits of a picture, just as it is always possible not to appreciate Shakespeare, or not to realise that novels contain insights. Anything approaching a 'proof' of such insight involves long and hard wrangling, under good conditions of communication, over particular cases. And this we cannot do here.

5

Mental health and educational practice

'Curing' and 'educating'

These two concepts, between which we made a sharp distinction earlier (pp. 8-9), have been brought somewhat closer together by our more recent discussion (pp. 57-63). The distinction is of importance chiefly because 'curing' implies abnormality due to malfunction, whereas 'educating' does not. 'Education', as has been clearly demonstrated by other writers (Peters, 1966) 'is a matter of *initiating* people into various worth-while activities'. But this does not necessarily imply either (a) that the people you educate are, so to speak, like blank sheets of paper with regard to the mental activities—that their minds are totally unformed or un*in*formed about them: nor (b) that the kind of way their minds do work in these activities—what is written on the paper already, so to speak—is perfectly satisfactory and 'rational', as opposed to just being rather ignorant or deficient: that is, they may already have false, irrational or distorted ideas and attitudes.

The point here is that there is no intrinsic difference between the *methods* of the educator and the teacher on the one hand, and someone who is concerned with 'curing' those who are mentally ill *in the way we have described* on the other. There is a difference of method *only* when the 'mental illness' is of the kind that can be remedied without the 'patient' having to relearn: by drugs, surgery, or whatever. The method is then different, because 'education' entails helping people to learn, and excludes carving them up or giving them pills. But the kind of mental ill-health we have been talking about is not in this category: it involves helping a person to relearn, to regain touch with reality, to behave more rationally, and so forth.

Of course this does not mean that this curative activity includes the *whole* of education, or that 'mental health' can be regarded as the sole object of educating people. Even though, according to our picture, it may be plausible to say that most people are mentally unhealthy, they are not unhealthy in every aspect of their behaviour or their thinking. Education adds to or enlarges the individual consciousness, whether or not the individual is mentally unhealthy: it increases rationality in certain fields of study whether or not the student was irrational before he started to learn. Education may teach me more about negroes, whether or not I was racially prejudiced to begin with. Nevertheless, the curative activity we are discussing is methodologically like education: it may be directed towards the same ends as education: and it may certainly find a place in education. How important a place this should be we will consider later.

It is in a way unfortunate that all aspects of 'mental health' have been lumped together under the same name, and that it is hard to avoid using words like 'cure', or 'patient'. This tempts us to oppose 'teachers' to 'doctors', 'ordinary people' to 'patients', and 'educate' to 'cure'. For, in fact, many teachers and parents, and indeed individuals in general, do engage in activities which are 'curative' in just this way. They reason with each other, and with the children in their care, help them to try to see how other people feel, attempt to show them their own feelings, create warm atmospheres in which they may talk more freely about their personal relationships, and so on. What they do is not substantially different from what psychiatrists do: and yet the image of a psychiatrist or a psychoanalyst as a special sort of doctor, a 'head-shrinker' with magic powers, still persists. There are various reasons, psychological as well as social, for the continued power of this image, into which we cannot go now.

Because of the power of this image, some readers may feel let down. They may feel, in effect: 'Oh, well, all you're talking about is helping children with their personal problems, making them feel less anxious, getting them to be more reasonable, giving them more love and security, and so forth. All that's fine, but why drag in mental health?' But I hope to have shown that, if we set our sights at the right level, we cannot avoid the view that most or all children are mentally unhealthy in a way which precisely requires that these activities—too casually referred to as 'helping children with their problems', etc.—should be taken very seriously, both in schools and elsewhere. *Of course* one can describe, not only curative measures for this kind of mental ill-health, but the whole secret of bringing up children, the whole of Christianity, indeed the whole art of living, by the single word 'love'. But this hardly does justice to the nature of the problem (the mislearning of childhood), or to the possibilities that we might consider for solving the problem in actual educational institutions.

Before we go further, however, we must certainly not forget our distinction between the two types of mental health; and I do not at all want to create the impression that mental ill-health caused by physical factors, or deficiencies that have to be remedied by experts, is unimportant. In this book we cannot consider such cases in detail, though it is easy for the reader to pursue the matter for himself if he has a specialised interest in it. Obviously, all teachers must at least be able to recognise and identify such cases, and willing to bring them to the notice of the authorities: and where there is inadequate provision for them, it will no doubt be useful for the teacher to have some idea of how to handle them himself. But the proper identification and care of such cases is inevitably an expert matter.

Two further points also arise.

Of course teachers are not psychiatrists, and cannot be entirely trained as such. To that extent, they may often have to refer cases of mental ill-health of the kind in which we are particularly interested—that is, cases of mislearning—to psychiatric experts. Often the teacher may be unable to make any progress with such cases at all: often too he will wonder whether what he does is harmful rather than useful. To stress the importance of this aspect of mental health is not to say that teachers either can, or should try to, 'do the psychiatrists out of a job'.

Further, the teacher may be obliged to display a certain general attitude towards his pupils—let us say, one of respect, benevolence and (non-passionate) love—without *always* being obliged to act as a psychiatrist and try to remedy their mental ill-health. There is no need to say much about this general attitude, since I assume that it is a desideratum in all forms of teaching, not only in helping children to relearn and improve their rationality in the way already described. I think, however, that the teacher who is personally concerned with his pupils as people will find it hard to prevent his love or benevolence from spilling over into some sort of attempt to improve their rationality. One must not forget the distress and suffering caused by mental ill-health of this kind. It would be a hard-hearted teacher indeed who, if a child was pathologically anxious or frightened, persisted in drumming irregular verbs into his head without bothering to ask him why he was anxious or frightened. Yet even to notice this, and certainly to ask for the reasons of it, is already to be involved in the sort of curative activity we are discussing. Children do not often show such obvious symptoms as this: if they did, even those teachers who are not 'psychologically-orientated' might take notice. And a teacher who is prepared to use his eyes, and look at the child as well as the child's exercise-book, will easily see symptoms of malfunction which may persist in later life if he does not help the child to overcome it.

Mental health and the curriculum

There are at least four ways in which mental health is important for a school. One of these is not primarily connected with the notion of a 'curriculum', but rather concerns such questions as the arrangements of the school as a social institution, the personality of the teachers, extra-curricular activities, and so forth. This we shall leave to a later section. The other three are as follows.

As a necessity before subject-learning. Mental health, up to some standard or other, is plainly a precondition of learning. If the child cannot sit still, is worried about his parents, has a 'mental block' against mathematics or reading, etc., we have to remove these symptoms if he is to make any progress in the subject taught. Regrettably but predictably, it is usually very difficult to remove a particular symptom without thereby causing another symptom to arise in its place; and if the symptom arises from mislearning (rather than from some other cause), it is (in my view) always impossible. All we can do is to help the child to learn better; and this takes time. To increase rationality cannot be done by terrorism, indoctrination, or machinery: though any of these, and other methods too, can be used to put the child in a state in which he can *begin* to learn.

In other words, we have here the usual dichotomy. If the symptoms are like toothache, or fits, or attacks of vertigo, we may be able to remove them—and hence establish the necessary preconditions of his learning a subject—by dental operations or drugs. But very often children confront a subject with symptoms of the other kind of ill-health. Perhaps they unconsciously associate counting and mathematics with a fierce father who beat

68

them for not giving the right change: or perhaps, to use a rather fantastic-sounding Freudian-type explanation, learning to read or puzzle out the 'secrets' of a book unconsciously reminds them of a terrifying curiosity about the sexual activities of their parents when they saw them in bed together. Whatever the reasons—and they need not be as complicated as this—we can only remove the symptoms by discovering them, and getting the child to face reality without these unconscious and irrational terrors.

Very often the symptoms concern not the subject as such, but features of the teaching situation in general. Most teachers will have noticed, for instance, the markedly different attitude which different children have to books. Some will show an immediate and lively interest in what is inside the book, and are initially disposed to regard the book as 'good', 'helpful', 'interesting', etc.: others, who may be said to suffer from deficiency rather than malfunction, look on books as if they were just bits of wood, perhaps because their parents showed a similar lack of interest: others again have an irrational attitude due to some malfunction, and regard them with positive suspicion, as if they were in some way magic objects or taboo. Again, and even more obviously, the way in which children react to the teacher as a person differs greatly. Some children are immediately aggressive, others are constantly demanding attention, others again are too anxious to placate, and so forth. Similar symptoms may be seen in older children, with reference to their fellow-pupils or 'peer groups' as well as to the teacher.

There are of course few cases where a child, even if his mental illness is in fact quite severe, will make absolutely *no* progress in a subject. But in almost all cases the rate of progress is, I would guess, as much determined by the rationality or irrationality of his basic attitudes as by any other factor. The preconditions of learning at a reasonable speed, therefore, are very closely connected with mental health; and indeed a stronger and more coherent attack on mental ill-health may cause us to expect a much greater rate of progress than that which we are now satisfied with. Even now one is tempted to interpret the 'bright boys', who seem to find no difficulty in mastering their subjects, as those whose minds are not blocked or distorted in some way, rather than (as we usually do) as those who have some special 'genius', 'talent', or 'high I.Q.' in which the rest of the class is just deficient. What we commonly refer to as 'problem-solving' or 'intelligence' may thus be more a matter of mental health than innate ability.

As entailed by certain subjects. The aspect of mental health we are chiefly concerned with may already have suggested to the reader a close connection with some activities already established in the educational curriculum. It is possible to draw a very rough distinction between those subjects which involve skills and perceptions similar to those in virtue of which a person is mentally healthy, and those which require only a very basic level of mental health. For example, mathematics and science do, of course, involve a degree of psychological rationality, in that a complete lunatic, or someone who kept contradicting himself, could not prosper in them. Such things as care, attention to detail, ability to remember facts and so forth are also important. But it is no discredit to mathematics or science to say that they do not involve us in the necessity for insight or perception of human beings. They are not concerned with personal relationships, or inner feelings, or what other people thought or said. Much mathematics and science could be taught by machines.

On the other hand, a great many 'arts' subjects are so concerned. To take the outstanding example of literature, we can easily see how any real progress in this discipline must depend on the child's ability to enter into the lives of the fictional characters, to understand as much as he can of their thoughts and feelings, and so forth. In history

70

too, he must learn how to think and feel like (say) a person in Victorian England or classical Greece. At the early stages, these subjects will naturally include a great many 'brute facts'—grammar, spelling, historical dates, and so forth—which could also be taught by machines, or which indeed he could look up in a reference book. But the essence of the subjects lies in insight and perception.

Such insight and perception is directly related to mental health, in that we inevitably tend to see other people (in the past or in novels) in our own terms. Understanding other people and understanding ourselves are intimately connected. Thus, to take a primitive example, the child who, for psychological reasons of his own, has an irrational admiration for all conquerors and tyrants will be unlikely to appreciate the history of democratic Athens: and the teenager whose attitude to religion is extremist will hardly understand the history of the Crusades. Similarly, one might hope that a girl would grow out of an all-embracing passion for love stories with happy endings, and a boy out of an exclusive preference for Westerns or war stories. But they will only do this if they can develop normally; and such normal development is not only a matter of initiating them into higher forms of literature. It is also a matter of getting them to shed their prejudices and their fears, so that they can see the interest of tragedies or of novels in which hardly anyone gets killed. Or to put it another way, initiating them into literature is itself partly a matter of removing their distorted vision.

Where this kind of teaching is well done, it is often difficult to say whether the teacher is 'teaching mental health' or 'teaching literature': and I have tried to show that this dichotomy is a false one, inasmuch as the latter may include the former. To teach them well, a close communication with the pupils is necessary, and the form of a dialogue is often more useful than the form of a lecture. The good teacher characteristically identifies his pupil's feelings and prejudices, and adjusts or adds to them: he

71

says, for instance, 'Perhaps you feel that Antony was a "good" man and Cleopatra just "wicked": yes, but look at this passage in the play, is he really being "good" or is he just trying to impress people . . .?' and so on. The work being done here is not unlike that of the psychiatrist.

As a focus for new subjects. Many people in the educational world today are, as we noticed in chapter 2, concerned to develop aspects of the child's personality and abilities which, they believe, our existing curricula fail to cover. This concern may express itself in many forms and under many titles: 'learning to live', 'personal relationships', 'moral education', and so forth. What we have said about mental health adds some weight to this concern; and it is not unreasonable to believe that we may use the notion of mental health as a focus for the creation of new subjects, disciplines or activities which would not normally fall under such headings as 'citizenship', 'social hygiene', etc.

I do not wish to say much about how this concern would most profitably be formalised in schools, since the reader may more easily read about this elsewhere. But two points must be stressed. We are here concerned with the *curriculum*, rather than with general arrangements in the social life of the school. If we are going to invent new subjects or disciplines, we must first get clear about what these subjects *are*, what counts as doing them successfully, how we (and the children) are to know that progress is being made, and even—if possible—how they can be tested or examined. 'Mental health' is not something which children just pick up, as they might pick up an infection. The type or rationality which is the reverse of the kind of malfunctioning we are considering needs to be broken down into a clearer set of components and objectives.

However, this caution need not amount to despair. It is conceivable that, by using such methods as play-acting, showing films, discussion and so forth, children may learn to improve their ability to know what other people are feeling, which is plainly one of the kinds of rationality we have in mind. Other contexts may give them insight into their own feelings, into social roles, the way of life of inhabitants of other countries, adherents of other religions, and so forth. It is not too hard to see how we could test the judgements they made in these matters: and perhaps the more imaginative teacher may be able to think up methods for himself.

These new 'subjects' may, after all, not be *totally* new. Much that teachers now do by way of helping children in this direction reminds one of existing subjects in higher-level institution—psychology, sociology, philosophy, anthropology, and so on. We should not be frightened off by the mere names of these disciplines. Rather we should gain some notion of what the disciplines aim at, and try to use their methods and objectives for the benefit of children, in a way which suits the particular children we have to teach. Many of them are, in fact, not 'high-level' subjects in the sense that 'higher mathematics' is: that is, something which one can only do after having done the same subject at a lower level for many years. They are more like special skills, or approaches, to life which may be able to be learnt at an early age. The child who learns about how Eskimos live is already doing 'anthropology', and the teenager who learns about the problem of old people 'sociology' and 'psychology'.

A note on 'subjects'

In this context the word 'subjects' is usually taken to mean the areas of study normally covered at school—Latin, algebra, English, history and so forth. These areas of study are very loosely-defined (for instance, is there one subject 'classics' or two subjects, 'Latin' and 'Greek'?). A 'subject' in this sense, i.e. an area of study traditionally accepted, should not be confused with a particularly logical discip-

ECMH—F

line or form of understanding. Disciplines or forms of understanding differ from each other by making use of different concepts, and asking logically different questions which require different types of verification. (For an attempt to distinguish these forms of understanding, see Paul Hirst's article in R. Archambault's collection *Philosophical Analysis and Education*.)

It will be seen from this that the same form of understanding may enter into more than one subject, and also that a subject may be made up of more than one form of understanding. Thus the ability to understand oneself and other people is necessary for history, English literature and some kinds of sociology: and the subject 'history' is made up partly of this form of understanding, and partly of other forms (e.g. straightforward factual knowledge of dates).

Non-curricular factors

Here again, I fear we cannot spend too much time in considering details: but it will be worth our while to list some of the factors which seem likely to be relevant.

The personality of the teacher. This may well be a more important factor than those concerned with curricular subjects. Very little effective research has been done in this field; but it should be possible for the teacher to assess and understand his own personality, so that at least he may avoid the worst errors. As in the family, so in the school there is a kind of unconscious 'teaching' which goes on all the time; and for all the kinds of 'conscious teaching' we have mentioned in section B above, the teacher's personality is crucial.

But there is one particularly important point to be made here. We have concentrated on one particular aspect of mental health, that aspect which cannot be dealt with entirely by the *knowledge* of the specialist. We must stress 'knowledge', for it is here that the contrast between the 'scientific' and the psychiatric healer arises. If my ailment needs drugs or surgery, the personality of the doctor or surgeon does not matter much: what matters is whether he *knows* enough. But if my ailment is such that it needs someone to help me relearn—someone who will understand me as a person and not just as a machine—then that person's personality is all-important. Nor does this mean that he must be benevolent, patient, and so forth: it means that he must have sufficient personal *insight* to understand my case. Now this quality is itself closely related to our particular kind of mental health.

This is why the training of psychoanalysts includes a 'training analysis', in which their own mental health (and thus their insight) is improved. If teachers are to improve their own ability to deal with these particular cases of mental health, something like the same procedure must be adopted. This has an important bearing upon the training of teachers, and upon what teachers can do by their own efforts. The teacher who wishes to develop the specialised, 'scientific' expertise of being able to identify, and perhaps assist in curing, those cases of mental ill-health which are the product of specific physical causes, has one kind of task. But the teacher who wishes to deal with our particular kind has to develop insight; and this is not something he can learn wholly from books, as he can learn scientific facts from *books*.

The use of experts. The point we have just been discussing raises the question of how and when schools should make use of expert psychotherapists; for, of course, there are experts in this field, even if their expertise is different from that of the scientist. Part of the answer to this question must always depend on purely practical considerations: e.g. whether a good psychotherapist is actually available, what kinds of cases of ill-health there are at the school, how competent the teachers themselves are as amateur psychotherapists, and so forth; but one or two general points may be made.

First, we need in practice some mean between two extreme positions. We might feel, on the one hand, that these cases are so complex and important as always to need expert treatment. On this view, teachers should withdraw from their role as amateur psychotherapists altogether, and refer all such cases to the experts. On the other hand, we may feel that a properly-trained teacher with the right sort of personality should be able to handle most 'cases'—and not all those suffering from ill-health need be regarded in this extreme way—himself, as they arise, in the normal course of the school's functioning. Which of these is nearer the truth will depend on the actual facts, as we have just said : but it is important not to be initially prejudiced towards either extreme, by an over-serious or a superficial attitude respectively.

Secondly, it is probably beneficial both for mental health and for other educational desiderata that a reasonably sharp line should be drawn between treatment and teaching—in the child's mind, if not in the teacher's. The child needs a firm framework consisting of the school's expectations and rules, the demands made on him by reality, the standards he is expected to live up to. He must be able to measure himself against this, and realise that he needs help when he fails. There is, then, something to be said on these lines for the rather grim-sounding procedure of 'sending him to the psychotherapist', just as for the procedure of 'sending him to the headmaster'.

Thirdly, for anything approaching a serious case it is a necessary condition of treatment that the therapist should be, so to speak, a neutral figure : that is, *not* a person who has already generated certain expectations in the child, as would be the case with a parent, a housemaster, or a subject-teacher. The reasons for this are complicated, but amount to the fact that the child must, to be cured, somehow get *outside* or *behind* the network of reactions to expectations which he has already developed, and which is inadequate for the real world : he can only relearn with a neutral figure who does not make demands upon him. This is a further argument for the use of experts who are not already part of the pattern of school life.

Finally, however, it must be granted that a great deal can be done by those working in the school, precisely because they *are* part of the child's normal world. A child may form a close relationship with someone who impresses him—perhaps his form-teacher, his housemaster, games mistress, etc.—and who can, in consequence, use this 'transference' of the child's affections to help the child. Who these members of staff will be depends partly on them, and partly on how the school is organised. Thus, it was no doubt true that the school chaplain played a significant part, not unlike that of the psychiatrist, as 'father confessor'—a semi-neutral figure, partly connected with the 'establishment' forces in the school, but partly also one who was thought to be willing to deal with the individual's problems in a neutral fashion, even if his neutrality was coloured by a particular religious metaphysic.

Social arrangements in the school. This brings us to the third set of factors, which concern the way in which the school is organised in general. Of course no planned system will work unless the point is understood by the staff, and unless they are willing and capable of carrying out its objectives; but the organisation is necessary if willing and capable people are to have scope, and it is quite likely that most of the immediately beneficial changes may come in this area. It may be, in other words, that many schools already contain sufficient personnel to make a substantial improvement in the mental health of the schools' pupils, if only the system permitted and encouraged this.

We have only time to mention a few possibilities here,

some of which are already becoming actualised in various schools—mostly those who conceive their function more in 'mental health' terms and less in terms of passing examinations or maintaining their social status. Amongst these we may list:

(a) The importance of rituals that bind the community together, in the way that morning assemblies used to (and perhaps in some cases still do): or in the way that taking food together, for instance, may help to make the individual child feel more secure, as in a family.

(b) The importance of avoiding such an atmosphere of competition as will produce a class of under-privileged children who feel that they have failed: this involves more stress on co-operative activities, and so arranging the school activities that every child can feel that he is successful in some field.

(c) The importance of arranging activities that fit the age and nature of the child in his particular stage of development: for instance, sufficient opportunities for the release of aggression in adolescents, and for such sexual activities as developing children will be concerned with.

(d) The importance of allowing sufficient extra-curricular time and space to give the children a chance to express themselves, outside the class-room situation, under the eye of adults who may thus gain more insight into the children as individual *people*.

(e) The importance of decentralising the school, insofar as may be required, so that the child will have an identity as a member of a permanent group, attached to an adult, rather than feeling that he is lost in a vast, shifting structure where unknown people make sporadic attempts to teach him things.

These and similar points are perhaps obvious enough,

and may be pursued elsewhere (see Wilson, 1968). Much more research is of course needed before we can determine their relative importance. But the imaginative teacher will no doubt be able to judge, from his position on the inside of a particular school, what kinds of changes may be needed. As we have stressed more than once, however, he will only be able to do this effectively if he already has—or is prepared to develop—sufficient insight to perceive what the child's needs are : where the school structure is failing to correct, or may even be reinforcing, the mislearning which the child has done in his family background.

Liaison with the family. Ultimately, of course, the child's family background and history are all-important; and it would be absurd to think that the school can ever replace the family, either in regard to mental health or in other respects. We have to face the fact, however, that many families no longer fulfil adequately their proper function of giving the child that security and understanding in his early years which is so necessary. Perhaps, indeed, it is not that family life is worse than it was : it may be that the rapid changes in the modern world, and particularly the break-down in authority and in the acceptance of public norms and standards, have simply caught the ordinary parent unprepared. Until his preparation is more effective, therefore, the school has to help.

The problem of communication here is all-important. Anything that can be done by parent-teacher associations, by visits to the children's homes, by inviting the parents to take part in school functions, and by increasing the general understanding on both sides, is well worth doing. Schools that do this successfully often produce a remarkable loyalty on the part of the parents, and the child himself does not feel split into two, in the way that may easily happen if there is a division of loyalty between home and school. That somebody to whom he is attached *outside* the school should care what he does inside it is perhaps one of the most important aids to a child's general development.

Equally, however, the understanding teacher can help the child to compensate for the deficiencies of his home life. He can help him to understand his parents and himself better, and give him something of the warmth and affection which may be denied him at home. He can help the child to admire his parents, to reduce his conscious or unconscious hostility to them, to incorporate them into his life at school, and to show them that affection which they may little deserve, but which at some level will be inevitably felt by the child. The teacher can show that he understands the position and problems of his parents, and is sympathetic to them : and, in brief, that home and school are not two totally disconnected worlds.

A note on 'moral education'

I do not want to say very much about this topic, because I have written more fully about it elsewhere (Wilson, 1968). But the reader may like to bear the following points in mind :

1. The connection between mental health (in the sense discussed in chapter 4) and what may be called 'moral education' is very close : and the same holds good if we use such general titles as 'human relations', 'learning to live', 'personality-training' and so forth instead of 'moral education'. Not only does the making of rational moral judgements depend on awareness of the feelings of others, which we have seen to be an important aspect of mental health, but there is also a whole range of decisions which are 'moral', even if in a somewhat extended sense of the word, and which depend almost entirely on self-awareness and self-control. This range is indeed

co-extensive with 'mental health' as we have interpreted it. (Wilson, *op. cit.*, ch. 2.)

2. 'Moral education', like mental health, will not necessarily be something which we teach over the desk-tops at certain hours of the school day. It may be done partly by a subject-approach, and partly by the non-curricular arrangements mentioned above. Many of the suggestions made here will apply to moral education as well as to mental health (Wilson, *op. cit.*, Part III).

3. Just as mental health is not to be defined in terms of the views or practices of any particular individual or social group, so too moral education will not be a matter of getting children to conform to any particular *mores*: it will rather be a matter of giving them certain attitudes, skills, abilities and capacities which are required in order to be rational in the moral sphere (Wilson, *op. cit.*, ch. 1).

The reader must appreciate that we have here done little more than single out what are generally thought, by practising teachers as well as by psychological and other experts, to be some of the most important general factors of school life in relation to mental health. Some may well be questioned: others may be so vaguely-stated as to be little more than truistic. We are here in the middle of a subject where adequate research is only just beginning to be done, and which the reader needs to pursue for himself, learning both from the experts and from the actual practice of certain schools. Nobody can as yet speak with authority in this field.

I do not think, however, that an attitude of excessive caution is in place here. If various educational reformists (consider Barnardo, Pestalozzi, Montessori and many others both today and in the past) had held their hands until all the results of research were to hand, we should not even have been able to see just what the area was on which we needed more research. Caution is certainly required : but we need also a spirit of vigour and enthusiasm, the chief elements of which must be a concern for the child himself and a perceptive understanding of his needs as a person. Nothing is easier to say, and nothing harder— for some people, at least—to acquire.

6
Epilogue

In conclusion I would invite the reader to reflect on what he has read. In the Introduction we promised to explain how the concept of mental health was of importance to everybody, and not just to a number of experts. Has this promise been redeemed? In chapter 2 we examined some of the ways in which people commonly thought about 'mental health' under the influence of science, and briefly considered the ways in which these popular views were crystallised into the form which most educational institutions now have, and the objectives they pursued, with the resulting pressures on the teacher: and we concluded by asking ourselves how this existing situation might be amplified by other educational ideals. Was this picture a fair one? Does it show a confusion about the concept of 'mental health' which might stand in the way of new educational ideals?

In chapters 3 and 4, which formed the bulk of this book, we tried to do some hard thinking about concepts: to make clearer what was meant by 'ill', 'health', 'normal', 'adjusted' and so forth: and (in chapter 4) to outline one particular aspect of mental health which might cause us to revise our common ideas of 'normality' and 'health' in general. Did we succeed in becoming clearer about these concepts? Do we now feel more confident in being able to say what counts as 'mental health' and what does not? Is the picture painted in chapter 4 a convincing one? Is it as important as was there claimed?

Finally in chapter 5 we tried to apply the picture in chapter 4 to educational practice. How far do our suggestions tally with what we saw in chapter 4 and earlier in the book? Are we correct in the general conclusion that much more attention ought to be paid to this kind of 'mental health' in schools? What other measures could be suggested? What kind of research needs to be done?

If the reader is still uncertain about the answers to these questions—and it may well be that he *ought* still to be uncertain—he may, of course, profit from re-reading this particular work. But if I have done nothing else, I hope to have shown the importance of the questions; and nothing would be better than that the reader, as I have many times suggested, should pursue particular topics in books of a more profound and scholarly nature.

Yet one warning should be issued before we conclude. If the reader is to pursue such topics profitably, he must be clear exactly what sort of questions he wants to know the answer to. This particular book consists primarily of an analysis of concepts, or a clarification of meaning. Others are concerned with the facts of individual psychology, with the sociology of education, with specific topics within these ('The Retarded Child', 'The School as a means of Social Mobility', etc.), and so forth. The enquiring reader should always ask himself just what kind of talk, and what kind of questions, are to be found in any particular work. The 'subject' that we call 'education' today is methodologically very confused: and it is only by getting clear about the nature of the different disciplines that comprise it that the reader will find his questions answered adequately. Otherwise all that remains in his mind is a sort of nameless blur: a phenomenon with which teachers themselves, as well as those who train teachers, are only too familiar.

Bibliography

Here are a few books which the reader might find useful; of course there are many more, but I have tried to select those amongst the most readable as well as the most important. The first group is primarily concerned with conceptual or philosophical questions which are relevant to mental health, in the way that this book has been; the second group is concerned more generally with the kind of psychology relevant to mental health.

MACINTYRE, A. C. (1958) *The Unconscious*, London: Routledge & Kegan Paul. A conceptual analysis of the role of the unconscious in Freudian theory: a short and readable book dealing with a very complex problem.
PETERS, R. S. (1960) *The Concept of Motivation*, London: Routledge & Kegan Paul.
   (1964) 'Mental health as an Educational Aim', in HOLLINS, T. H. B., ed., *Aims of Education*, Manchester: Manchester University Press.
   (1965) 'Emotions, Passivity and the Place of Freud's theory in Psychology', WOLMAN, B., and NAGEL, E., *Scientific Psychology*, New York: Basic Books.

These works are concerned with the nature of the concepts of emotion, motive, rationality, and mental health, and represent the most important philosophical contributions to this general topic hitherto.

   (1966) *Ethics and Education*, London: Allen and Unwin. Perhaps the only really good general philosophical work on education. The later chapters are particularly relevant to the notion of rationality in various forms.

BIBLIOGRAPHY

WILSON, JOHN, *et al.* (1968) *Introduction to Moral Education*, London: Penguin Books. An attempt to lay the foundations for the whole topic of 'moral education': Part I is particularly relevant, and deals with the notion of rationality in relation to mental health as well as in relation to moral judgements.

WISDOM, JOHN (1953) *Philosophy and Psychoanalysis*, Oxford: Blackwell. A series of essays, written in an informal but illuminating style, which clarify the nature of different types of argument, proof and rationality, and shed much light on psychoanalytic-type theories in general.

FLUGEL, J. C. (1955) *Man Morals and Society*, London: Duckworth. A lengthy but very clear application of Freud's theories to the general topics of morality and the development of the individual.

FOULKES, S. H., and ANTHONY, E. J. (1965) *Group Psychotherapy*, London: Penguin Books. An account of the aims and practice of group therapy, from a Freudian viewpoint: of particular interest is the authors' use of communication as a basic concept.

FREUD, ANNA (1931) *Introduction to Psychoanalysis for Teachers*, London: Allen and Unwin. A short book which brings some of Freud's insights to bear on the practical work of the schoolteacher.

FREUD, S. (1962) *Two Short Accounts of Psychoanalysis*, London: Penguin Books.

MONEY-KYRLE, R. E. (1951) *Psychoanalysis and Politics*, London: Duckworth. An attempt to interpret political theory in the light of Freud's theories: the author is particularly concerned with the notion of a rational personality.

RYCROFT, CHARLES (1966) *Psychoanalysis Observed*, London: Constable. A collection of essays, many of which throw new and interesting light on the nature of psychoanalysis.

STORR, ANTHONY (1963) *Integrity of the Personality*, London : Penguin Books. A very clear and readable account of the criteria used in psychotherapy : in no way partisan, the author is more persuasive than many more committed psychologists.

WILSON, JOHN (1965) *Logic and Sexual Morality*, London : Penguin Books. An attempt to consider the rationale of sexual morality, partly from the philosophical point of view, and partly from general psychological and sociological observation.

The judgements made above about these books are purely my own, and, of course, disputable.

General editor's introduction

THE STUDENTS LIBRARY OF EDUCATION has been designed to meet the needs of students of Education at Colleges of Education and at University Institutes and Departments. It will also be valuable for practising teachers and educationists. The series takes full account of the latest developments in teacher-training and of new methods and approaches in education. Separate volumes will provide authoritative and up-to-date accounts of the topics within the major fields of sociology, philosophy and history of education, educational psychology, and method. Care has been taken that specialist topics are treated lucidly and usefully for the non-specialist reader. Altogether, the Students' Library of Education will provide a comprehensive introduction and guide to anyone concerned with the study of education, and with educational theory and practice.

This book provides a lucid examination of a number of concepts which we all frequently use in everyday discussion and which are of particular importance to parents and teachers—terms like ill, health, moral, maladjusted and so on. But the book is not only a discussion of theory, important as that is; the clarification of thought is used in the consideration of a number of practical issues including the organisation of the curriculum, the social arrangements in the school, moral education and relations between home and school. The book is also, therefore, from the student's point of view, an exercise in conceptual analysis and the kind of philosophic thinking which is advocated in the introductory volume, *The Study of Education*.

J. W. TIBBLE

First published 1968
by Routledge & Kegan Paul Ltd
Broadway House, 68-74 Carter Lane
London, E.C.4
Printed in Great Britain
by Northumberland Press Limited
Gateshead

© John Wilson 1968

SBN 7100 6221 4 (C)
SBN 7100 6158 7 (P)

Education and the Concept of
Mental Health

by John Wilson
Director of the Farmington Trust Research Unit, Oxford

LONDON
ROUTLEDGE & KEGAN PAUL
NEW YORK: HUMANITIES PRESS